FREE Test Taking Tips Video/DVD Offer

To better serve you, we created videos covering test taking tips that we want to give you for FREE. **These videos cover world-class tips that will help you succeed on your test.**

We just ask that you send us feedback about this product. Please let us know what you thought about it—whether good, bad, or indifferent.

To get your **FREE videos**, you can use the QR code below or email freevideos@studyguideteam.com with "Free Videos" in the subject line and the following information in the body of the email:

    a. The title of your product

    b. Your product rating on a scale of 1-5, with 5 being the highest

    c. Your feedback about the product

If you have any questions or concerns, please don't hesitate to contact us at info@studyguideteam.com.

Thank you!

MPRE Study Guide
2 Practice Tests and MPRE Exam Prep Book
[Includes Detailed Answer Explanations]

Lydia Morrison

Written and edited by TPB Publishing.

TPB Publishing is not associated with or endorsed by any official testing organization. TPB Publishing is a publisher of unofficial educational products. All test and organization names are trademarks of their respective owners. Content in this book is included for utilitarian purposes only and does not constitute an endorsement by TPB Publishing of any particular point of view.

Interested in buying more than 10 copies of our product? Contact us about bulk discounts: bulkorders@studyguideteam.com

ISBN 13: 9781637757758

Table of Contents

Welcome

Dear Reader,

Welcome to your new Test Prep Books study guide! We are pleased that you chose us to help you prepare for your exam. There are many study options to choose from, and we appreciate you choosing us. Studying can be a daunting task, but we have designed a smart, effective study guide to help prepare you for what lies ahead.

Whether you're a parent helping your child learn and grow, a high school student working hard to get into your dream college, or a nursing student studying for a complex exam, we want to help give you the tools you need to succeed. We hope this study guide gives you the skills and the confidence to thrive, and we can't thank you enough for allowing us to be part of your journey.

In an effort to continue to improve our products, we welcome feedback from our customers. We look forward to hearing from you. Suggestions, success stories, and criticisms can all be communicated by emailing us at info@studyguideteam.com.

Sincerely,
Test Prep Books Team

FREE Videos/DVD OFFER

Doing well on your exam requires both knowing the test content and understanding how to use that knowledge to do well on the test. We offer completely FREE test taking tip videos. **These videos cover world-class tips that you can use to succeed on your test.**

To get your **FREE videos**, you can use the QR code below or email freevideos@studyguideteam.com with "Free Videos" in the subject line and the following information in the body of the email:

> a. The title of your product
> b. Your product rating on a scale of 1-5, with 5 being the highest
> c. Your feedback about the product

If you have any questions or concerns, please don't hesitate to contact us at info@studyguideteam.com.

1

Quick Overview

As you draw closer to taking your exam, effective preparation becomes more and more important. Thankfully, you have this study guide to help you get ready. Use this guide to help keep your studying on track and refer to it often.

This study guide contains several key sections that will help you be successful on your exam. The guide contains tips for what you should do the night before and the day of the test. Also included are test-taking tips. Knowing the right information is not always enough. Many well-prepared test takers struggle with exams. These tips will help equip you to accurately read, assess, and answer test questions.

A large part of the guide is devoted to showing you what content to expect on the exam and to helping you better understand that content. In this guide are practice test questions so that you can see how well you have grasped the content. Then, answer explanations are provided so that you can understand why you missed certain questions.

Don't try to cram the night before you take your exam. This is not a wise strategy for a few reasons. First, your retention of the information will be low. Your time would be better used by reviewing information you already know rather than trying to learn a lot of new information. Second, you will likely become stressed as you try to gain a large amount of knowledge in a short amount of time. Third, you will be depriving yourself of sleep. So be sure to go to bed at a reasonable time the night before. Being well-rested helps you focus and remain calm.

Be sure to eat a substantial breakfast the morning of the exam. If you are taking the exam in the afternoon, be sure to have a good lunch as well. Being hungry is distracting and can make it difficult to focus. You have hopefully spent lots of time preparing for the exam. Don't let an empty stomach get in the way of success!

When travelling to the testing center, leave earlier than needed. That way, you have a buffer in case you experience any delays. This will help you remain calm and will keep you from missing your appointment time at the testing center.

Be sure to pace yourself during the exam. Don't try to rush through the exam. There is no need to risk performing poorly on the exam just so you can leave the testing center early. Allow yourself to use all of the allotted time if needed.

Remain positive while taking the exam even if you feel like you are performing poorly. Thinking about the content you should have mastered will not help you perform better on the exam.

Once the exam is complete, take some time to relax. Even if you feel that you need to take the exam again, you will be well served by some down time before you begin studying again. It's often easier to convince yourself to study if you know that it will come with a reward!

2

Test Taking Strategies

1. Predicting the Answer

When you feel confident in your preparation for a multiple-choice test, try predicting the answer before reading the answer choices. This is especially useful on questions that test objective factual knowledge. By predicting the answer before reading the available choices, you eliminate the possibility that you will be distracted or led astray by an incorrect answer choice. You will feel more confident in your selection if you read the question, predict the answer, and then find your prediction among the answer choices. After using this strategy, be sure to still read all of the answer choices carefully and completely. If you feel unprepared, you should not attempt to predict the answers. This would be a waste of time and an opportunity for your mind to wander in the wrong direction.

2. Reading the Whole Question

Too often, test takers scan a multiple-choice question, recognize a few familiar words, and immediately jump to the answer choices. Test authors are aware of this common impatience, and they will sometimes prey upon it. For instance, a test author might subtly turn the question into a negative, or he or she might redirect the focus of the question right at the end. The only way to avoid falling into these traps is to read the entirety of the question carefully before reading the answer choices.

3. Looking for Wrong Answers

Long and complicated multiple-choice questions can be intimidating. One way to simplify a difficult multiple-choice question is to eliminate all of the answer choices that are clearly wrong. In most sets of answers, there will be at least one selection that can be dismissed right away. If the test is administered on paper, the test taker could draw a line through it to indicate that it may be ignored; otherwise, the test taker will have to perform this operation mentally or on scratch paper. In either case, once the obviously incorrect answers have been eliminated, the remaining choices may be considered. Sometimes identifying the clearly wrong answers will give the test taker some information about the correct answer. For instance, if one of the remaining answer choices is a direct opposite of one of the eliminated answer choices, it may well be the correct answer. The opposite of obviously wrong is obviously right! Of course, this is not always the case. Some answers are obviously incorrect simply because they are irrelevant to the question being asked. Still, identifying and eliminating some incorrect answer choices is a good way to simplify a multiple-choice question.

4. Don't Overanalyze

Anxious test takers often overanalyze questions. When you are nervous, your brain will often run wild, causing you to make associations and discover clues that don't actually exist. If you feel that this may be a problem for you, do whatever you can to slow down during the test. Try taking a deep breath or counting to ten. As you read and consider the question, restrict yourself to the particular words used by the author. Avoid thought tangents about what the author *really* meant, or what he or she was *trying* to say. The only things that matter on a multiple-choice test are the words that are actually in the question. You must avoid reading too much into a multiple-choice question, or supposing that the writer meant

3

something other than what he or she wrote.

5. No Need for Panic

It is wise to learn as many strategies as possible before taking a multiple-choice test, but it is likely that you will come across a few questions for which you simply don't know the answer. In this situation, avoid panicking. Because most multiple-choice tests include dozens of questions, the relative value of a single wrong answer is small. As much as possible, you should compartmentalize each question on a multiple-choice test. In other words, you should not allow your feelings about one question to affect your success on the others. When you find a question that you either don't understand or don't know how to answer, just take a deep breath and do your best. Read the entire question slowly and carefully. Try rephrasing the question a couple of different ways. Then, read all of the answer choices carefully. After eliminating obviously wrong answers, make a selection and move on to the next question.

6. Confusing Answer Choices

When working on a difficult multiple-choice question, there may be a tendency to focus on the answer choices that are the easiest to understand. Many people, whether consciously or not, gravitate to the answer choices that require the least concentration, knowledge, and memory. This is a mistake. When you come across an answer choice that is confusing, you should give it extra attention. A question might be confusing because you do not know the subject matter to which it refers. If this is the case, don't  eliminate the answer before you have affirmatively settled on another. When you come across an answer choice of this type, set it aside as you look at the remaining choices. If you can confidently assert that one of the other choices is correct, you can leave the confusing answer aside. Otherwise, you will need to take a moment to try to better understand the confusing answer choice. Rephrasing is one way to tease out the sense of a confusing answer choice.

7. Your First Instinct

Many people struggle with multiple-choice tests because they overthink the questions. If you have studied sufficiently for the test, you should be prepared to trust your first instinct once you have carefully and completely read the question and all of the answer choices. There is a great deal of research suggesting that the mind can come to the correct conclusion very quickly once it has obtained all of the relevant information. At times, it may seem to you as if your intuition is working faster even than your reasoning mind. This may in fact be true. The knowledge you obtain while studying may be retrieved from your subconscious before you have a chance to work out the associations that support it. Verify your instinct by working out the reasons that it should be trusted.

8. Key Words

Many test takers struggle with multiple-choice questions because they have poor reading comprehension skills. Quickly reading and understanding a multiple-choice question requires a mixture of skill and experience. To help with this, try jotting down a few key words and phrases on a piece of

4

scrap paper. Doing this concentrates the process of reading and forces the mind to weigh the relative importance of the question's parts. In selecting words and phrases to write down, the test taker thinks about the question more deeply and carefully. This is especially true for multiple-choice questions that are preceded by a long prompt.

9. Subtle Negatives

One of the oldest tricks in the multiple-choice test writer's book is to subtly reverse the meaning of a question with a word like *not* or *except*. If you are not paying attention to each word in the question, you can easily be led astray by this trick. For instance, a common question format is, "Which of the following is…?" Obviously, if the question instead is, "Which of the following is not…?", then the answer will be quite different. Even worse, the test makers are aware of the potential for this mistake and will include one answer choice that would be correct if the question were not negated or reversed. A test taker who misses the reversal will find what he or she believes to be a correct answer and will be so confident that he or she will fail to reread the question and discover the original error. The only way to avoid this is to practice a wide variety of multiple-choice questions and to pay close attention to each and every word.

10. Reading Every Answer Choice

It may seem obvious, but you should always read every one of the answer choices! Too many test takers fall into the habit of scanning the question and assuming that they understand the question because they recognize a few key words. From there, they pick the first answer choice that answers the question they believe they have read. Test takers who read all of the answer choices might discover that one of the latter answer choices is actually *more* correct. Moreover, reading all of the answer choices can remind you of facts related to the question that can help you arrive at the correct answer. Sometimes, a misstatement or incorrect detail in one of the latter answer choices will trigger your memory of the subject and will enable you to find the right answer. Failing to read all of the answer choices is like not reading all of the items on a restaurant menu: you might miss out on the perfect choice.

11. Spot the Hedges

One of the keys to success on multiple-choice tests is paying close attention to every word. This is never truer than with words like *almost*, *most*, *some*, and *sometimes*. These words are called "hedges" because they indicate that a statement is not totally true or not true in every place and time. An absolute statement will contain no hedges, but in many subjects, the answers are not always straightforward or absolute. There are always exceptions to the rules in these subjects. For this reason,

you should favor those multiple-choice questions that contain hedging language. The presence of qualifying words indicates that the author is taking special care with his or her words, which is certainly important when composing the right answer. After all, there are many ways to be wrong, but there is only one way to be right! For this reason, it is wise to avoid answers that are absolute when taking a multiple-choice test. An absolute answer is one that says things are either all one way or all another. They often include words like *every*, *always*, *best*, and *never*. If you are taking a multiple-choice test in a subject that doesn't lend itself to absolute answers, be on your guard if you see any of these words.

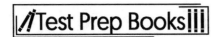
12. Long Answers

 In many subject areas, the answers are not simple. As already mentioned, the right answer often requires hedges. Another common feature of the answers to a complex or subjective question are qualifying clauses, which are groups of words that subtly modify the meaning of the sentence. If the question or answer choice describes a rule to which there are exceptions or the subject matter is complicated, ambiguous, or confusing, the correct answer will require many words in order to be expressed clearly and accurately. In essence, you should not be deterred by answer choices that seem excessively long. Oftentimes, the author of the text will not be able to write the correct answer without offering some qualifications and modifications. Your job is to read the answer choices thoroughly and completely and to select the one that most accurately and precisely answers the question.

13. Restating to Understand

Sometimes, a question on a multiple-choice test is difficult not because of what it asks but because of how it is written. If this is the case, restate the question or answer choice in different words. This process serves a couple of important purposes. First, it forces you to concentrate on the core of the question. In order to rephrase the question accurately, you have to understand it well. Rephrasing the question will concentrate your mind on the key words and ideas. Second, it will present the information to your mind in a fresh way. This process may trigger your memory and render some useful scrap of information picked up while studying.

14. True Statements

Sometimes an answer choice will be true in itself, but it does not answer the question. This is one of the main reasons why it is essential to read the question carefully and completely before proceeding to the answer choices. Too often, test takers skip ahead to the answer choices and look for true statements. Having found one of these, they are content to select it without reference to the question above. The savvy test taker will always read the entire question before turning to the answer choices. Then, having settled on a correct answer choice, he or she will refer to the original question and ensure that the selected answer is relevant. The mistake of choosing a correct-but-irrelevant answer choice is especially common on questions related to specific pieces of objective knowledge.

15. No Patterns

One of the more dangerous ideas that circulates about multiple-choice tests is that the correct answers tend to fall into patterns. These erroneous ideas range from a belief that B and C are the most common right answers, to the idea that an unprepared test-taker should answer "A-B-A-C-A-D-A-B-A." It cannot be emphasized enough that pattern-seeking of this type is exactly the WRONG way to approach a multiple-choice test. To begin with, it is highly unlikely that the test maker will plot the correct answers according to some predetermined pattern. The questions are scrambled and delivered in a random order. Furthermore, even if the test maker was following a pattern in the assignation of correct answers, there is no reason why the test taker would know which pattern he or she was using. Any attempt to discern a pattern in the answer choices is a waste of time and a distraction from the real work of taking the test. A test taker would be much better served by extra preparation before the test than by reliance on a pattern in the answers.

Introduction

Function of the Test

The Multistate Professional Responsibility Examination (MPRE), developed by the National Conference of Bar Examiners, is a requirement for admission to the bars of nearly all U.S. jurisdictions (excluding Wisconsin and Puerto Rico). It's administered three times per year by the NCBE's test contractor, Pearson VUE.

Test Administration

The MPRE is only available to take each March, August, and November, but it's important for test takers to submit their registration for the test at least four months in advance. Registering for the MPRE is a multi-step process that first requires an online account with NCBE. On the account, test takers can register for a session of the MPRE as well as request reasonable accommodations in accordance with the Americans with Disabilities Act.

If the request is approved, the test taker will be sent an Authorization to Test email from Pearson VUE around 24 hours after applying. After receiving the authorization, the test taker will need to schedule an appointment with Pearson VUE and pay the test fee.

Test takers can expect to receive their scores within five weeks of taking the MPRE. The scores will be viewable on the test taker's online NCBE account, and they'll remain available until the next test is administered (usually around four months). Test takers can also choose to have their scores sent to them in an unofficial score transcript, or to have their scores reported to a jurisdiction.

Test Format

The MPRE is a two-hour, 60-question computer-based test that measures test takers' understanding of how lawyers should conduct themselves professionally. Although only 50 of the questions are scored and 10 are unscored pretest questions, the pretest questions are indistinguishable from the actual test questions. Therefore, test takers should answer every question as if it were to be scored.

Each question on the MPRE is a multiple-choice question with four answer choices. Test takers will not lose points for incorrect answers, so it's better to guess than leave a blank answer.

Scoring

The scores for the MPRE range from a low of 50 to a high of 150. Each state sets their own passing score, which ranges from 75-86 across the different jurisdictions. The average test taker's MPRE score in 2023 was 96.6, which is a passing score in every jurisdiction.

Questions on the MPRE come from the 12 domains, or subjects, including in its' scope of coverage. Each domain composes a certain percentage of the MPRE test questions, which can be found in the table below:

Domain	Percentage	Questions
Domain I: Regulation of the Legal Profession	6-12%	4-7 questions
Domain II: The Client-Lawyer Relationship	10-16%	6-10 questions
Domain III: Data Insights	6-12%	4-7 questions
Domain IV: Conflicts of Interest	12-18%	7-11 questions
Domain V: Competence, Legal Malpractice, and Other Civil Liability	6-12%	4-7 questions
Domain VI: Litigation and Other Forms of Advocacy	10-16%	6-10 questions
Domain VII: Transactions and Communications with Persons Other Than Clients	2-8%	1-5 questions
Domain VIII: Different Roles of the Lawyer	4-10%	2-6 questions
Domain IX: Safekeeping Funds and Other Property	2-8%	1-5 questions
Domain X: Communications About Legal Services	4-10%	2-6 questions
Domain XI: Lawyers' Duties to the Public and the Legal System	2-4%	1-2 questions
Domain XII: Judicial Conduct	2-8%	1-5 questions

Study Prep Plan for the MPRE

1 **Schedule** - Use one of our study schedules below or come up with one of your own.

2 **Relax** - Test anxiety can hurt even the best students. There are many ways to reduce stress. Find the one that works best for you.

3 **Execute** - Once you have a good plan in place, be sure to stick to it.

One Week Study Schedule		
Day 1	Domains I-III	
Day 2	Domains IV-VI	
Day 3	Domains VII-IX	
Day 4	Domains X-XII	
Day 5	Practice Test #1	
Day 6	Practice Test #2	
Day 7	Take Your Exam!	

Two Week Study Schedule			
Day 1	Regulation of the Legal Profession	Day 8	Different Roles of the Lawyer
Day 2	The Client-Lawyer Relationship	Day 9	Safekeeping Funds and Other Property
Day 3	Client Confidentiality	Day 10	Communications About Legal Services
Day 4	Conflicts of Interest	Day 11	Lawyers' Duties to the Public and the Legal...
Day 5	Competence, Legal Malpractice...	Day 12	Practice Test #1
Day 6	Litigation and Other Forms of Advocacy	Day 13	Practice Test #2
Day 7	Transactions and Communications with...	Day 14	Take Your Exam!

9

One Month Study Schedule							
Day 1	Regulation of the Legal Profession	Day 11	Competence, Legal Malpractice, and Other Civil Liability	Day 21	Lawyers' Duties to the Public and the Legal System
Day 2	Regulation of the Legal Profession	Day 12	Litigation and Other Forms of Advocacy	Day 22	Lawyers' Duties to the Public and the Legal System
Day 3	The Client-Lawyer Relationship	Day 13	Litigation and Other Forms of Advocacy	Day 23	Judicial Conduct
Day 4	The Client-Lawyer Relationship	Day 14	Take a Break!	Day 24	Judicial Conduct
Day 5	Take a Break!	Day 15	Transactions and Communications...	Day 25	Take a Break!
Day 6	Client Confidentiality	Day 16	Different Roles of the Lawyer	Day 26	Practice Test #1
Day 7	Conflicts of Interest	Day 17	Safekeeping Funds and Other Property	Day 27	Answer Explanations #1
Day 8	Conflicts of Interest	Day 18	Communications About Legal Services	Day 28	Practice Test #2
Day 9	Take a Break!	Day 19	Communications About Legal Services	Day 29	Answer Explanations #2
Day 10	Competence, Legal Malpractice...	Day 20	Take a Break!	Day 30	Take Your Exam!

Build your own prep plan by visiting:

testprepbooks.com/prep

Domain I - Regulation of the Legal Profession

A. Powers of Courts and Other Bodies to Regulate Lawyers

The American Bar Association (ABA) is a group of lawyers and law students that establishes and organizes the ethical rules and standards for the practice of law in the United States. These ethical codes of conduct were written and revised to form the current *Revised Model Rules of Professional Conduct* that now serves as the foundation for ethics in the law profession. The rules consist of definitions and instructions lawyers are expected to follow in order to be fair to both state law and the clients they represent as well as to develop a professional standard to monitor lawyers and judge their abilities to effectively perform their duties. The rules also include a section for comments by the ABA to clarify and help lawyers interpret and apply each rule to their specific cases. Each section of the *Model Rules* is intended to serve as a tool to formally ensure specific ethical codes are followed when practicing law, preventing subversive or harmful acts by lawyers who might take advantage of those who are not in the profession. The *Model Rules* forms the basis many states choose to use to regulate lawyers.

Many states use the *Model Rules* to establish their own system for regulating lawyers. Therefore, those entering the legal profession can get a general idea of the standards lawyers are expected to maintain and practice by reading and understanding the *Model Rules*. However, each state may also adopt different or additional regulations that are intended to be followed when working in their specific jurisdiction. The state government's published set of ethical rules for lawyers are the ultimate guidelines for regulating conduct of those in the profession, so when there is a difference between the *Model Rules* and the state's rules, the state's rules will ultimately be the ones that are enforced. These enforcements are then conducted by the state's court system, often with help from the ABA.

B. Admission to the Profession

Applying to become a lawyer in most states requires a bachelor's degree in any discipline (business or political science are popular options), a law school degree, an application with direct references to the state for which one is applying, and a passing score on the Multistate Professional Responsibility Examination and bar exam. Applications should include the applicant's complete background check, work history, and educational background. Any terminations from past employers or gaps in employment should also be truthfully stated. Past guilty convictions of crimes need to be provided and explained as well. The law is written and understood through scrupulous attention to detail; therefore, lawyers working with state law need to also be able to provide detailed information regarding their qualifications to represent and/or work with those who create the laws.

It is important to only submit truthful information with a bar application in order to avoid disciplinary action after admittance. The ABA created its *Model Rules* to ensure that those entering the profession know the ethical guidelines and can maintain a level of professionalism expected when becoming a lawyer. When attempting to enter the profession, it is important to understand the obligations and duty one has to the law and the courts. Admission requires adherence to all state law regulations and open discussions of these regulations with clients to ensure a level of understanding and trust is given to the practicing lawyer by the client and the court. A lawyer needs to have a complete understanding of the rules of both their state and the federal government before applying for the bar. Those who willingly make false statements when applying to become a lawyer will likely do the same when representing clients; therefore, any false statements need to be corrected and removed or changed before admission

11

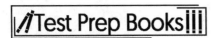
to the legal profession. References used from others in the profession for admission should also be free from untrue or misleading information about the character of the applicant. The ABA will conduct investigations on all those involved if they believe an individual was admitted to the bar based on false claims.

C. Regulation After Admission—Lawyer Discipline

After admission to the profession, a lawyer is regulated by the state through their judicial system, the ABA, or both. Lawyers who break the code of conduct for ethics are subject to the disciplinary action of those in charge of enforcing regulations for the profession. A lawyer may also be disciplined for misrepresenting the profession as a whole, either through dishonesty or malpractice, to be determined by the state. Also, helping another lawyer break a rule or work unscrupulously will lead to disciplinary action. The state creates these rules to protect its citizens from lawyers who may not have their clients' best interests in mind when representing them or who may willingly act unjustly for personal profit without the knowledge of those they are representing. Lawyers who discriminate against individuals based on race, sex, religion, age, etc., are also subject to discipline to maintain the integrity of the profession.

A lawyer suspected of misconduct or malpractice will be subject to an investigation, either by the state that administered the lawyer's bar exam or the state where the infraction occurred. If, after the investigation, the lawyer is convicted with proof that they broke the rules of the state regarding the practice of law in their jurisdiction, the lawyer will be subject to punishments that might incorporate suspensions from a certain practice or outright suspension of their entire practice. Some cases may also result in the complete removal of the individual's ability to practice law.

D. Mandatory and Permissive Reporting of Professional Misconduct

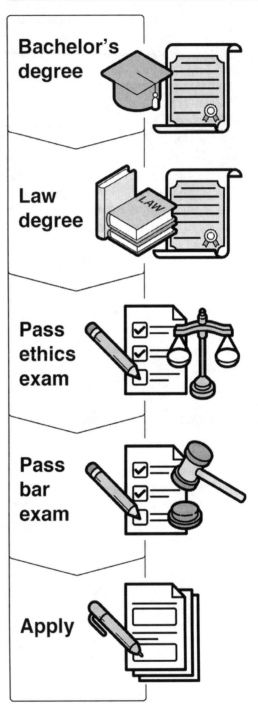

Steps to Become a Lawyer

Bachelor's degree

Law degree

Pass ethics exam

Pass bar exam

Apply

The *Model Rules* established by the ABA specifies that every lawyer admitted to the profession is required to report any misconduct or breach of ethics that might violate the rules. This reporting should, however, be regulated to specific situations in which there is proof that misconduct has occurred because in any ensuing investigation, all parties will need to provide this proof as to why another lawyer

12

acted unethically in a given situation. The situation also should be important enough to warrant investigation, determined by whether or not the action caused harm to the parties involved. For example, a lawyer who charges a high rate for a service that could be done for much less is not enough cause to report, but if the lawyer willingly made up information to charge the client extra, the case would warrant reporting. Lawyers are obligated to maintain a level of confidentiality about each case they work on; however, this confidentiality can and should be broken if harmful misconduct is observed. A lawyer can obtain a consent of disclosure from their client if they believe their case information is essential to reporting misconduct, as long as it does not go against the client's best interests.

A lawyer can report misconduct to the ABA, which has a specific committee designated to investigate situations and administer disciplinary action. States may have their own agency dedicated to reporting misconduct as well, so it is important to check the jurisdiction's regulatory procedures to ensure the correct steps are taken. All lawyers need to be aware of their colleague's actions to help stop misconduct that could diminish the influence of their profession and cause public distrust in the system. Although a lawyer is not necessarily required to report their own misconduct, the practice of monitoring other lawyers' conduct ensures the profession as a whole is kept fair and just for clients and professionals.

E. Unauthorized Practice of Law—By Lawyers and Nonlawyers

When a lawyer practices law, they are using their knowledge of the rules and regulations created by their state's judicial system as well as logical deductions and their best judgment according to how they interpret the facts of a particular situation to correspond with this law in order to make decisions in an active case. **Practicing** in this case refers to using the law in specific instances to pass a judgment or interpret a situation that requires action on the part of the court. The lawyer is practicing law when they are making deductions about how to utilize the law to best fit their client's interests. Only those accredited by the bar as professional lawyers are allowed to practice law in this manner. However, it is not considered practicing law when information is simply researched and organized in a way that assists the lawyer in practicing law; nonlawyers are legally allowed to perform these actions for a real case under the guidance and observation of a professional lawyer. An **unauthorized practice of law** would constitute a nonlawyer making decisions in a case.

Unauthorized practice of law also occurs when lawyers practice law when their license has been suspended or revoked or in a state in which they are not licensed. If a lawyer wished to practice law in another jurisdiction they do not have the time to be licensed in, they need to either work with a lawyer who has the proper authorization to practice in the area or obtain temporary permission from the local court authority by filing the correct paperwork. If a lawyer engages in unauthorized practice, they could be criminally charged and face fines and potential imprisonment depending on the severity of the situation. They may also not be allowed to practice law in the future if found guilty of unauthorized practice.

F. Multijurisdictional Practice

Because each state has its own established set of bar requirements, a lawyer is only permitted to practice law in the state from which they obtained their bar certification. However, sometimes a lawyer may need to travel to another state to represent a client and therefore would need a way to practice law in that state without being subjected to the punishments of unauthorized practice. This might happen during a personal injury case in which the incident occurs in a state outside of where the client

lives. Most states require an injury case to be filed in the place where the injury occurred, so the lawyer would need to find an exception to the rule of practicing law in the state where the lawyer was certified.

One way for a lawyer who is practicing a case of federal law to qualify to practice in multiple jurisdictions would be to apply for admission to the state court by filing the corresponding state's admission forms. Some states also use a uniform bar exam that acts as a general admission to transfer a lawyer's general admission bar score to each state where they wish to practice. Other states also collaborate to allow lawyers from each state to work in any of the other states that have agreed to allow the practice. Lawyers can also work with a lawyer who is admitted by the state bar where they wish to practice, as long as both lawyers actively participate in the work.

G. Fee Division with a Nonlawyer

In general, according to the ABA's *Model Rules,* lawyers are not allowed to share, distribute, or divide legal fees with a nonlawyer. This is to ensure that a client's case is not split among different parties that are not required to represent their best interests. However, the *Model Rules* does list several exceptions to this rule. The first includes what might happen to fees after a lawyer's death, in which case, after a period of time, the fees could be allocated to someone named by the lawyer in a previous agreement. Another rule specifies an instance in which a lawyer might pay the purchase price to a specified party for a practice of someone who no longer practices law.

As for employees who work with the lawyer on a specific case they receive fees for, the lawyer is only allowed to use fees obtained to create a compensation or retirement plan for their employees; they cannot simply divide the fees among their staff if they are not lawyers. However, if the lawyer works with a nonprofit organization that recommends them for a case, the lawyer is allowed to divide the fees with the organization. No other circumstance would allow fee division with nonlawyers, and any lawyer who distributes these fees in a way that is not authorized will be subjected to disciplinary action, including suspension or revocation of their ability to practice law in the jurisdiction.

H. Law Firm and Other Forms of Practice

Most lawyers work out of law firms that specialize in specific aspects of the law. When studying law, a lawyer must choose a certain type of law to specialize in, which will determine the type of firm the lawyer will most likely join. Law firms come in various sizes, from large corporate organizations to small practices with only one or two lawyers. They may also cover only one specific area or represent a larger number of jurisdictions. Specialized law firms might only work with corporations, and some will only handle criminal cases. Large firms might hire a team of lawyers and paralegals with different specialties to work with a wide range of clients. The type of specialty will determine the work performed, but all cases will require the work of a team of professionals, each working under a lawyer, who in turn works under the firm.

Cases require large amounts of work to be performed, from paperwork to meetings to research, and some law firms may not have enough of a workforce to complete all the required tasks on time. In this case, there are other forms of practice referred to as **alternative legal service providers**, or organizations that firms outsource legal work to for help with a case. Alternative legal service providers are often highly specialized groups of law professionals that can support law firms with their expertise. These organizations can also help clients with quick cases, such as trademark filings or business licensing, that do not need the full support or time of a law firm to complete. However, all organizations

that offer legal services will conduct day-to-day operations in a slightly different way; therefore, when determining the best business or firm to work for as a lawyer, it will ultimately be up to how much one feels they are welcome and helpful to their team while working cases.

I. Responsibilities of Partners, Managers, Supervisory and Subordinate Lawyers

It is the responsibility of all those working with the law to follow their state's guidelines for correct conduct and upholding the moral responsibilities of the law profession. Partners, managers, supervisory lawyers, and subordinate lawyers all must ensure they are following the rules put in place for representing clients at all times. **Partners** are individuals who work with a lawyer or law firm on specific areas of a case. Their responsibility is to the client and the state, just like the lawyers. They are expected to provide information and services to the firm they are working with to the best of their abilities. If a partner is given managerial roles or certain authority over others in a firm, they must act the same way a manager of the firm would act. The **manager** of a law team is in charge of implementing and enforcing rules that have been created by the organization to maintain an ethical practice. Therefore, the manager is responsible for any malpractice they may commit as well as any committed by the employees they supervise.

The **supervisory lawyer** is often the lawyer who is in charge of the subordinate lawyers or paralegals of a law firm. The supervisor needs to make sure all their subordinates understand and can reasonably act under the ethical code established by the firm and the state. They must also ensure that none of their instructions are unethical or could be determined as malpractice. However, the subordinate lawyer is responsible for acting under their superior's instruction only as far as it is legal and ethical. Whereas the supervisor is ultimately responsible for the actions of their subordinates, the **subordinate lawyer** also needs to be aware of what they are doing and have enough general knowledge of the law to determine when their actions or their colleagues' actions might break the law or be considered unethical.

J. Restrictions on Right to Practice

The ABA currently forbids lawyers from entering into any form of agreement that restricts their right to practice. The rule was created to prevent cases from being settled on the promise that a lawyer will no longer bring about future cases on a defendant. This is an unethical practice because the lawyer is restricting their own right to do what their job requires: to practice the law. Any settlement that deals with a lawyer's ability to practice their profession should not be made or discussed by a lawyer, not only pertaining to their own ability to practice in the future but also in relation to an opposing lawyer during a settlement. This means that as part of an agreement, the lawyer representing their client cannot come to an arrangement with both parties if part of that agreement includes prohibiting either party's lawyer from representing that client or taking part in that particular client's cases at a later date. For example, a client cannot agree to settle a dispute only on the condition that the prosecuting attorneys promise not to bring any more charges against them in the future.

Often, several different but related cases may be brought against one individual by the same group of attorneys. In this instance, the individual may want to try and restrict others from the ability to bring about new cases and continue prosecuting them. However, due to the rules against the restrictions on the right to practice, no lawyer representing this client may try and deter future litigation.

15

Domain II - The Client-Lawyer Relationship

A. Formation of Client-Lawyer Relationship

The formation of a client-lawyer relationship establishes a commitment between a lawyer and the client, creating the scope and desired outcome of the duties a lawyer must perform for the client. After formation of the relationship, the lawyer is responsible for representing the client's best interests using the ethical guidelines created by the state. The lawyer is also expected to keep all information given to them by their client confidential unless they have consent from the client. As soon as the relationship is formed, the lawyer is obligated to help the client to the best of their ability under the scope of the law and finish their case.

A client-lawyer relationship starts when a client informs a prospective lawyer that they intend to hire them for a specific case. In this instance, any information exchanged relating to the case becomes confidential, even if the client decides to use a different lawyer. Just a proposition between a lawyer and a client can be considered a relationship, so it is important that a lawyer always remember their state's ethical code when speaking with a perspective client. A lawyer must also be sure to fully communicate their intentions to represent or not represent a client after information is exchanged. If a lawyer does not inform the individual who gave them information that they cannot represent them before they are able to reasonably find someone else, they have an obligation to enter a relationship with the individual and help them with their case. A court may also appoint a lawyer to a specific client prior to the client exchanging information, which in this situation would form a mandated relationship the lawyer must honor. No matter which way a client-lawyer relationship is formed, the lawyer must uphold the relationship by representing their client to the full extent of their abilities.

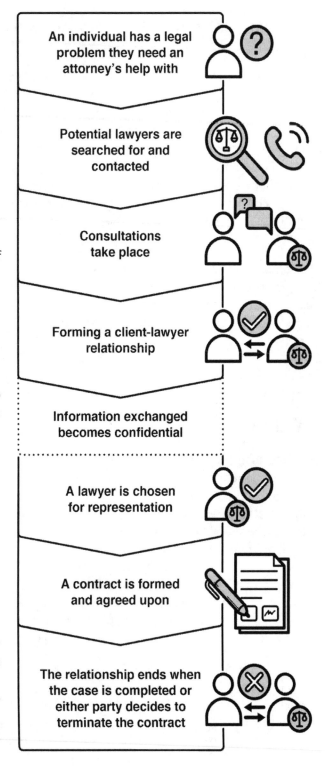

An individual has a legal problem they need an attorney's help with

Potential lawyers are searched for and contacted

Consultations take place

Forming a client-lawyer relationship

Information exchanged becomes confidential

A lawyer is chosen for representation

A contract is formed and agreed upon

The relationship ends when the case is completed or either party decides to terminate the contract

B. Scope, Objective, and Means of the Representation

A client and a lawyer need to set the scope, objective, and means of representation before commencing work to clearly establish what is to be accomplished for a specific case. Although choices are ultimately up to the client when deciding upon the scope of representation, the lawyer and the client will have a discussion to determine the goal to be achieved. Clients may only have a vague idea of how they should act in a given situation to fit their best interests, so it is up to the lawyer to describe the exact scope of services they are able to offer. Even if the scope or goals change during the case, as long as the lawyer and client are able to communicate consistently and effectively, they can come to an agreement about what direction would be the most advantageous within the boundaries of the law. Most jurisdictions require lawyers to consult regularly with their clients to fully understand and come to an agreement about what is to be accomplished.

Sometimes a lawyer may not be qualified or have enough time or funds to accomplish the entire scope of a client's request. When this happens, the lawyer may only work one specific aspect of a case or only work during a short amount of time. A lawyer can limit the scope of their representation if they have a rational reason the client understands and agrees to. However, if a lawyer and client agree beforehand on a specific objective and means of representation, the lawyer must follow through with their agreement to the best of their abilities; they cannot limit their scope of representation after they have already agreed to accomplish objectives that fall under the settled-upon scope.

C. Decision-Making Authority—Actual and Apparent

The client has the ultimate decision in certain situations, but in some circumstances the lawyer is permitted to make decisions on matters the client defers to them. **Actual authority** describes the instances in which the client must make the ultimate decision. For civil cases, the client has actual authority over deciding to settle a dispute or not. For criminal cases, the client has actual authority over how they want to plead, if they want to testify, or whether or not they want to have a trial by jury. The lawyer may give advice on these matters, but they are forbidden from making these decisions for their clients, notwithstanding certain specific circumstances. For instance, if the client is mentally unable make their own decisions, the lawyer can use their best judgment in the circumstance and make an actual authoritative decision based on the client's best interests.

Apparent decision-making authority includes all decisions that do not fall under the category of actual authority, which can be decided upon by the lawyer if the client gives consent. A client might feel unsure as to what decision would help them in complicated matters of the law that a lawyer may be more knowledgeable of. In these instances, the client can decide to give their lawyer authority over making decisions. It is also important to keep in mind that the lawyer must always act in the client's best interest when given apparent decision-making authority.

D. Counsel and Assistance Within the Bounds of the Law

A lawyer acts as both counsel and assistant to their clients, advising them on what can be done to achieve their goal, or stepping in and making decisions based on their knowledge of the law and the client's best interests. A lawyer can provide legal counsel to a client regarding the law pertaining to any question or problem a client may have. Lawyers can also provide help with legal documents and counsel individuals on tax issues or copyright laws. A lawyer is even permitted to provide counsel to individuals who have confessed to committing crimes or express a will to commit a crime in the future in the form

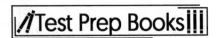

of explaining how their actions may be punished by the law. However, a lawyer is never allowed to help a criminal commit an act that knowingly breaks the law, and no counsel can be given to individuals who request the attorney to perform illegal activities. A lawyer must keep all practices within the bounds of the law.

A lawyer also cannot assist clients in any circumstance they believe to be in violation of the law. Helping a criminal to escape or commit an offense is a clear violation of the ethical code set for those who practice the law. If a lawyer believes the client they are representing is engaging in illegal activities, they may not continue to assist the client and have the right to forfeit any contract made before the illegal activities were committed or realized. A client can be given assistance without their expressed consent, however, when they are believed to be incapable of making rational decisions for themselves. This might happen if a client has a mental disability or is of a very young age. The lawyer, in these cases, is permitted to assist the client by making decisions for them to act in their best interest. However, no matter who the client is, a lawyer may never participate in any illegal counseling or assistance.

E. Termination of the Client-Lawyer Relationship

There are several circumstances that could terminate a client-lawyer relationship. The first would be if the work being requested violates the rules set out by the state for practicing law. Requiring a lawyer to perform illegal activities or give consultation for crimes would constitute an instance in which a lawyer should terminate their relationship with the client. A lawyer can also terminate the client relationship if they become seriously mentally or physically ill or are injured in a way that prevents them from completing their client's objectives. A client can terminate a lawyer at any time as well, no matter the circumstance. If a client decides the lawyer is not performing their job adequately for any reason, if they no longer need assistance, or even if they simply dislike the lawyer, they are permitted to end the relationship, as they make the final decisions regarding what the relationship should accomplish.

If a lawyer decides to end a client-lawyer relationship, they must have good reason and give their client enough time to find other representation. A lawyer must also ensure that, when ending a relationship, they have done what they can to ease the transition to another attorney or provide reparation for any problems that may have resulted in the separation. However, if ending the relationship would result in no adverse effects for the client, a lawyer is permitted to stop providing consultation and assistance if they desire, even if they have no particular reason. Also, a lawyer can end any relationship at any time if they believe their client desires assistance in committing a crime or if they feel the client is being unreasonably violent and rude to them. A lawyer has every right to stop providing legal counsel to those who are blatantly discriminatory or who try to bring harm to them or their legal team.

F. Client-Lawyer Contracts

Contracts between lawyers and clients are made to establish the type of work to be performed and at what price. It is an agreement that states in writing what the cost will be for each type of service, what work the client wants done, who will be in charge of completing the work, and how disputes will be settled, including how additional costs will be paid if incurred. Some contracts might also include what situations would constitute a breaking of the contract or bring about an end to the relationship. Rules for how the relationship should be conducted are also often included in contracts to establish consistent communication and guidelines to ensure lawyers are performing their job to the best of their abilities or for requiring clients to provide as much information as possible to the lawyer.

A written contract is not required in all circumstances, but, at the very least, a verbal agreement of services rendered and for what price needs to be established to create a client-lawyer relationship. Lawyers and clients both are bound to what they agree to and sign in their established contracts, so it is important to go over and approve every detail before contracts are finalized. After a contract is complete, it is the lawyer's duty to follow the requests of the client and fulfill the objectives that have been agreed to be paid for in exchange for completion. Unreasonable termination of a contract could result in legal fines for a client and possible suspension or revocation of the right to practice law for an attorney.

G. Communications with the Client

A lawyer is expected to maintain a consistent amount of contact with a client regarding their legal situation. Lawyers are also expected to clearly communicate with clients when actual decision-making authority is required, such as whether or not to settle a case, what to plead, to testify (when given the option), or to go to a trial by jury (if given the option). During these situations, the lawyer must always communicate with the client to find out what decision they wish to make in the matter. The lawyer can provide advice regarding what the consequences of these decisions may be, but ultimately, they must listen to what the client decides on these matters and do as instructed. Even if a lawyer believes they are more knowledgeable about the situation and can make a decision that would best benefit the client, the client still needs to be consulted regarding these important resolutions.

In other situations that do not require direct client decision making, the lawyer is not permitted to maintain constant contact with the client unless stated in a previously agreed-upon contract. The lawyer does, however, need to make sure their client is receiving all the relevant legal information relating to their case. Periodic communication with the client is also necessary to understand exactly what they want to accomplish. Keeping up with regular communication will help the lawyer understand the intentions of the client better, allowing the lawyer to make certain decisions without consultation when given permission. Basic aspects of a client's case and the laws pertaining to the situation should also be explained to clients so that a mutual understanding of what needs to be completed is established. A lawyer should avoid withholding information from the client unless instructed by the court; this way, the client always has at least a basic understanding of their situation and the possible outcomes of their case. The client should also be informed of any new information they could benefit from regarding their case when discovered.

H. Fees

Lawyers charge for their services in multiple ways, either through flat fees, hourly rates, or percentages of winnings, referred to as **contingency fees**. Most lawyers usually charge hourly rates for their work, including prices separated between lower-cost paralegal work and higher costs when the lawyer themselves does the work. Flat fees are used by more prestigious lawyers with a set of regular clients, whereas contingency fees are used for certain civil disputes. Their prices depend on the amount of work required, the amount of skill or knowledge required to perform the work, and the type and length of the case. A high-profile criminal case would merit a larger fee than a minor civil dispute, and a longer, ongoing case would of course cost more than a quick document filing. Where the lawyer works is also a factor, as the market demand for legal fees might be higher in certain areas. A more prestigious lawyer is also justified in charging higher rates than lawyers who have yet to prove their success.

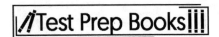

Although lawyers are expected to charge fees for legal work, the ethical code set out by the American Bar Association (ABA) requires that they do not charge unreasonable fees for services that do not demand the level of work required to justify the expense. Contingency fees require contracts to be written and signed before they are paid because clients can be easily taken advantage of in certain situations. Contingency fees are not allowed in certain domestic disputes and all criminal cases. However, except for contingency, other fees do not have to be written; they can simply be discussed between the client and lawyer and, if agreed upon, must be paid on time if the work is being completed, regardless of the outcome of the case.

Domain III - Client Confidentiality

A. Attorney-Client Privilege

The **attorney-client privilege** was established to allow clients to discuss legal matters with their attorney without the fear that what is discussed will be used against them. It allows clients to be completely up front with their lawyers about their situation, giving as much detail as they can for the lawyer to be able to fully help and accomplish agreed-upon goals. If the law team from the opposing party was to find this information through recordings or emails, they would not be able to use any of the information in their case against the client, no matter how incriminating, because the information would be protected by the attorney-client privilege. It also protects clients from accidently sacrificing their case by letting information that could aid their opposition be discovered.

Attorney-client privilege only exists between a lawyer and their client after a relationship has been established; no additional parties can be involved or informed of confidential information that is exchanged. The communication must also take place while the lawyer is actively working as an attorney on the case, and the dialogue must be for the purpose of obtaining assistance with a legal matter. The attorney-client privilege does not exist when discussing matters other than what the attorney was hired to accomplish. The attorney-client privilege can also be broken if the client discloses confidential information to another party that is not representing them, such as their friends or family, even if they are trying to help the client. Even if the third party only overhears the discussion when accompanying the client at a meeting with the attorney, the privilege would be broken because another person would have been given the information at the client's will. Also, like most agreements between a client and attorney, the privilege can be broken if the discussion is for assistance in breaking the law. Additionally, the attorney-client privilege can be waived by the client at any time if they desire the confidential information to be known in order to help their case.

B. Work-Product Doctrine

The **work-product doctrine** exists to protect the information lawyers compile and document for a case from being used against their client. Lawyers document important evidence and research that might be of use to their clients; these documents might contain incriminating information that could cause a client to lose their case if obtained by their opponent, so the work-product doctrine gives lawyers the freedom to create doctrines of information or other case-associated information without the fear of it being obtained and used by their opposition. Work-product doctrines include notes, folders, interviews, speeches, documents, or any written or spoken direct evidence relating to a case. Any work produced by the lawyer's team of assistants and paralegals can be considered a work-product doctrine as well and is also protected. However, documentation that was made before a client-lawyer relationship began or information that is not directly related to a client's case would not be protected under the work-product doctrine. The work would have to be produced for or during a client-lawyer relationship.

A lawyer is forbidden from using an opposing attorney's work-product doctrine to form their own strategy based on what their opponents have written or documented as well. However, if the information is absolutely necessary to solving a dispute and a lawyer's documents prepared for the case are the only way this information can be obtained, the work-product doctrine can be broken. Some information cannot be left out of a case if it is imperative to understanding the facts, and the court can determine that some documents would need to be disclosed in order to make a just decision.

Nevertheless, an attorney must be able to prove that the information is essential to the case, and the only way the information can be obtained is through inspection of the work-product doctrine of another attorney.

C. Professional Obligation of Confidentiality—General Rule

The general rule of **professional obligation of confidentiality** requires that any information relating to a case disclosed by a client to their lawyer after a lawyer-client relationship has been established be kept confidential. A lawyer is not allowed to discuss anything related to a client's case unless given explicit permission. This includes detailing any spoken or written statements about a case and any details that might be related to anything spoken or written by the client. The lawyer is obligated to ensure their client's objectives are not compromised by revealing important information that could be used against them. The rule is also used to establish trust between the attorney and client, giving the client the confidence to fully explain all the details of their situation to their attorney without fear that the information will be used by their opponents.

The rule is considered general because it encompasses any information that might be exchanged between a lawyer and a client. This includes the rules of attorney-client privilege that protects statements made by the client from disclosure and the work-product doctrine that protects documents created by the lawyer or their team to assist with understanding and winning a case. The rule also extends to after the case has ended and there is no longer any client-lawyer relationship. According to the professional obligation of confidentiality's general rule, when a lawyer agrees to represent a client or give them legal advice, they are agreeing to keep their evidence private as long as it can still be used in a dispute. The only instances in which the general confidentiality rule can be broken is if the client willingly gives permission to disclose the information.

D. Disclosures Expressly or Impliedly Authorized by Client

A client is entitled to openly express their desire to disclose confidential information at any point during a case, even if it may diminish their chance of success. In order for this information to be disclosed, the client needs to have an open discussion with their attorney about what information they want to release. A document might sometimes also be created and signed, confirming the client's request to disclose information generally protected by the professional obligation of confidentiality. Either way, the lawyer must discuss with their client the implications and possible outcomes if the information is released. All available options need to be explained to the client to ensure they have a full understanding of the implications of their choice. However, once the decision is made by the client, the lawyer must consent to any expressly authorized disclosure.

Impliedly authorized disclosure of confidential information occurs when a lawyer reveals information that would fall under the general rule of professional confidentiality without the expressed consent of the client. Because so much information is exchanged between parties in a case, it can be difficult for an attorney to continually seek out and ask for expressly authorized consent for every discussion about a case. The objectives are clearly stated when forming the lawyer-client relationship, and therefore the attorney should already have a clear grasp of what their client wants to accomplish. As long as the lawyer can justify that they were acting out of the best interests of the client, they can use implied disclosure to gain advantages in a case. This could include revealing information to aid a defense of the client or to discuss details of a case between their own law team, as they would all be under the same confidentiality agreement. However, if a client decides they do not want certain information disclosed,

22

the lawyer must respect the client's wishes and under no circumstances reveal the information the client does not want shared.

E. Other Exceptions to the Confidentiality Rule

The American Bar Association (ABA) created several exceptions to the confidentiality rule that are considered to be reasonable in certain situations. If the information can be used to prevent the harm or death of their client, the attorney is permitted to disclose the confidential information to help save the client. In addition, if the information relates to the undertaking of a crime or any illegal activity, the lawyer is permitted to disclose the information that would help stop the crime from occurring. If the client is telling their lawyer to assist them with causing harm, either physical, mental, or financial, to another party in an act forbidden by the law, the lawyer can break the confidentiality rule and disclose the harmful information to a third party. If the information given to the lawyer by a client can remedy any harm illegally caused by the client, the lawyer is also permitted to disclose the information to help mitigate the damage.

An attorney can also disclose confidential information to the authorities who create the ethical standards in their jurisdiction to help determine if the information should be released. A lawyer might be unsure as to whether or not they should disclose information, and asking others for clarification of the rules is permitted to avoid illegally releasing confidential details about a case. If the jurisdiction determines that the attorney is required to share the confidential details with the court, the lawyer must comply with what the court authorities instruct. Also, if there is a dispute between the client and lawyer, the lawyer is entitled to release confidential information to justify their actions or protect their reputation. If a client claims a lawyer acted wrongfully when representing them, the attorney has the right to defend themselves with information discussed during their client-lawyer relationship.

Domain IV - Conflicts of Interest

A. Current Client Conflicts—Multiple Clients and Joint Representation

Lawyers often take on multiple clients at a time to earn more income for themselves and their firm, allowing them to regulate costs for services. However, there are instances in which multiple cases might interfere with one another, causing one or both clients' cases to be compromised. If a lawyer gives confidential information about one case to another client, they are breaching one of their lawyer-client relationships. Additionally, if a lawyer gives preference to one client over the other, a conflict of interest would arise that would break the ethical code of conduct for practicing law. If a lawyer willingly takes on a client that is in opposition to a client they have already formed a relationship with, they are also creating a conflict of interest between the parties they represent. A lawyer is not permitted to take on two or more cases that are directly or indirectly related to each other in any way and, if over the course of representation, two cases become related or have the same parties involved, the lawyer must stop representing one of the clients to end conflicts of interest.

A conflict of interest can also happen if one client takes resources or time from another to the point where it adversely affects the client. When a lawyer accepts a case, they are committing to representing the client to their fullest ability, and if this ability is sacrificed by multiple parties, the lawyer may be breaking their contract. However, joint representation can occur if all parties involved have the same goals or are involved in a case against the same opponent. In this situation, an attorney can represent all parties because their interests are not conflicting and they are working toward similar goals. However, if a joint representation involves conflicting opinions or goals between two or more of the involved parties, there will be a conflict of interest and the lawyer would need to discontinue the joint representation.

B. Current Client Conflicts—Lawyer's Personal Interest or Duties

In addition to conflicts of interest between different clients, a lawyer's personal interests or duties can cause a conflict of interest if they affect their ability to fulfill their obligation to an individual or group they agreed to represent. There are multiple instances in which a lawyer's personal interests might impede their ability to represent their clients, and the American Bar Association (ABA) has detailed several of the most common instances and when these conflicts might occur. One example that might cause a conflict of personal interest would be if a lawyer advises a client to offer them some type of gift (of a significant amount or value) unrelated to fees accepted in the contract. The attorney also cannot ask for or draft documents that reward them or anyone they know with these types of gifts from their clients. However, minor gifts that are not meant to influence a case are acceptable. Additionally, a lawyer cannot gift a required fee to their clients, including court fines, meaning the lawyer cannot cover these fees and deem them a gift to the client. A lawyer may provide an advance on court costs, however, if they expect to receive compensation after the case has ended or from a settlement. If the individual is considered by the court to be financially unable to support themselves, the lawyer may also pay court fees with no expectation of return. Personal loans or monetary gifts are generally forbidden.

Personal relationships between lawyers or lawyers and their clients can also cause conflicts of interest. Unless agreed upon by the court and all parties involved, if a relationship exists between lawyers, an attorney cannot represent a client who is in conflict with a client their spouse or family member is

24

representing. Also, a lawyer and their client are prohibited from being involved in a personal, romantic relationship unless it existed before their lawyer-client relationship was formed.

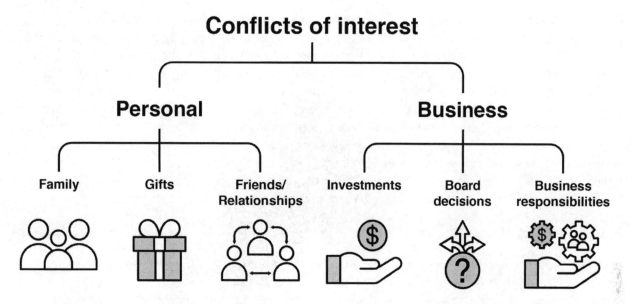

C. Former Client Conflicts

A lawyer is required to keep all information related to a case confidential unless given permission by the client, even after the case has ended and the lawyer-client relationship is over. This is because a former client's interests may interfere with those of a new client if the cases are related to the same dispute or involve similar parties. A lawyer is not allowed to take on a new client's case if it involves revealing confidential information gained from a previous client. The lawyer also may not represent an individual who has opposing interests to a client they represented in the past. The lawyer has an obligation to every client to always keep the information about their case confidential and never use it against them to help win a different case.

The former client conflict rules also apply to entire firms that might employ a large number of lawyers, each working with different clients. A lawyer cannot represent a client that has a conflict of interest with another client that is being or has been represented by the firm. Confidential information also cannot be distributed within the firm to benefit another client's or lawyer's interests. Former client conflicts can be relinquished, however, if the lawyer is able to receive, in writing, an agreement by the former client to do so. The only exceptions to the rule include if the information has become common knowledge or the jurisdictional authority allows the information to be disclosed for ethical reasons.

D. Prospective Client Conflicts

Prospective clients are individuals who have sought out legal counsel and are in the process of discussing and forming a relationship with an attorney but have not fully committed to a contract. This does not include general inquiries made to a law firm or unsolicited calls and emails; a client is prospective if they are meeting with a lawyer to discuss potential representation. Even though this individual has not become and may not become a client, the information they share with the attorney during a prospective meeting relating to a specific case they seek counsel for is considered confidential. A client needs to feel they are not hurting their case by giving information to a lawyer; therefore, there

is an established rule to allow them to confidentially disclose the full details of their case to an attorney to determine their ability to represent them.

A lawyer is also barred from knowingly representing another individual who is in opposition to a prospective client. This means that a lawyer or a law firm cannot receive confidential information from a prospective client and use that information when representing another party. However, only information that can be used to harm a prospective client is considered confidential in this case, and information that would not directly harm a client or their case can still be disclosed by a lawyer, even if they are not chosen to represent the client. Nevertheless, if a lawyer hears any information that might be harmful to disclose, they are no longer allowed to represent anyone who could use this information against the prospective client. This is why some lawyers may require written consent to disclose any information obtained in prospective meetings, or they may have another lawyer screen the individual, hearing the details of their case first. This way, the prospective lawyer does not directly hear any incriminating information that would disallow them from representing a different client.

E. Imputed Conflicts

Imputed conflicts deal with lawyers in a firm who represent a number of different clients at the same time. **Imputed conflicts** occur if one lawyer in a firm has a conflict of interest with a client another lawyer in their firm might be representing. Firms are not allowed to represent clients that might cause imputed conflicts. This is due to all the conversation that occurs between lawyers in a firm, making it likely that they might share confidential information another lawyer could use for personal benefit. Firms are considered similar to teams of lawyers in the way they often work together on cases and have the ability to easily access each other's documents. For this reason, no lawyer in a firm can represent a client that has a conflict of interest with any of the other attorneys in the firm. This rule extends to representing clients that have a conflict of interest with a lawyer who was previously working for the firm if their cases are connected.

One exemption to the imputed conflict rule exists if a lawyer only has a personal conflict of interest that is unrelated to the case. Also, if a lawyer has confidentiality obligations to a former client that might interfere with another attorney's case, the firm can still represent the client if they prohibit the lawyer from taking part in and receiving any payment from the case. The lawyer's former client must also be contacted and told of the potential conflicting interests and assured that their former attorney will not take part. The imputed conflict rule would also not apply to conflicts of interest between a client and a member of the firm who is not a lawyer, including assistants and paralegals.

F. Acquiring an Interest in Litigation

If a lawyer decides to represent a client, they are expected to work to accomplish the client's goals and interests in exchange for fees determined by the lawyer-client contract. An attorney is generally not allowed to work on cases that involve their own proprietary benefit outside of what they are being paid by the client or any contingency agreed to between parties. This rule was made to ensure lawyers are not overly invested in winning a case at the cost of sacrificing their client's requests or objectives. If a lawyer has too much personal interest in a case due to proprietary reasons, they are no longer representing the client. Rather, they are essentially representing themselves or their investments, which would break their obligation to work only for the client's best interests. It also makes the lawyer-client relationship more complex, becoming more difficult to sever if the situation is not beneficial to the client. A client has the right to end a case or dismiss a lawyer whenever they wish, but if a lawyer has a

26

significant interest in the case as well, they would more likely try to remain on the case without the client's consent, breaking the ethical requirements of attorneys set forth by the ABA.

Having a proprietary interest in a case is different from wanting to win a case for contingent fees. A lawyer is allowed to receive a percentage of settlements in a case if the numbers are agreed upon beforehand. The lawyer is also allowed to acquire a lien from the client as collateral for legal fees to be paid by contingency if discussed and accepted by the client and their attorney. In contrast, a proprietary interest would be more of an interest in compensation paid as a result of litigation rather than from clients for representation.

G. Business Transactions with Clients

Because lawyers have an extensive knowledge of the law, they are in a position to take advantage of clients that may not be as informed about the way settlements are rewarded or legal fees are determined. Clients are therefore given rights that protect them from a lawyer who might try to take advantage of them during business transactions. All business transactions between the client and attorney need to be agreed upon by both parties, with the client's full consent, and should be priced fairly according to the work requested.

One of the first steps in forming a lawyer-client relationship involves agreeing to the fees to be exchanged for a specific type of service. The lawyer and the client need to draft and sign documents, or at the least hold a discussion, that sets forth the scope of the case and the amount the client will have to pay for representation. If the client does not agree to all terms, the relationship is annulled. The client should also have as clear an understanding as possible as to where each fee might come from and what they will be expected to pay in contingency if included in the deal. There needs to be full consent of the terms before any payments can be made to protect the client from being charged for services they did not request. All fees should also be reasonable and match the going rates of other attorneys who offer similar services. A lawyer is not allowed to exploit charges for their own benefit, even if they believe the client will pay them. The relationship between the client and lawyer is based on trust that the lawyer is on their side and will not try to manipulate their agreement for personal gain.

H. Third-Party Compensation and Influence

Some clients may decide to have their legal fees paid by a third party who is designated to compensate the attorney instead of directly paying themselves. A business, friend, family member, or another party is permitted to compensate their relation's attorney as long as it is agreed upon by the attorney and client. A lawyer should not expect to receive compensation from a third party if it has not first been discussed and/or written into a contract that someone other than the client will be paying the legal expenses of their case. However, it is important to keep in mind that the attorney's loyalty is to their client at all times, not to a third party, even if the third party is the one paying the legal fees. The client always has the ultimate decisions in their case, and a lawyer's action should be directed at helping the client, not the interests of the third party.

The lawyer is also still required to uphold the same confidentiality obligations and conflict of interest regulations with a client even if they are not directly paying the attorney. The third party should still not be given any information related to the client's case, and all information exchanged in the private confidence of a lawyer and their client should continue to be kept between lawyer and client only. The client also still has the right to end the relationship at any time they desire, as they still have the

ultimate authority over their own case. The lawyer must refrain from allowing a third party's interests to affect their client's case. Conflicts of interest that might arise between a client and the third party should not interfere with the attorney's ability to do the best they can to represent their client. The lawyer should never go against their client's back by only adhering to the objectives of the different individuals responsible for paying them. No matter where the payments come from, the attorney's first priority is to represent only their client's best interests.

I. Lawyers Currently or Formerly in Government Service

Lawyers can work in many different firms during their careers, including both privately owned firms and government agencies. If a lawyer is currently working for the government, they are subjected to the same confidentiality and conflict of interest obligations as lawyers who work for private clients. A former private attorney who enters government service is barred from representing any government client that has an incident related to any past private case or who could possibly benefit from information learned during a past private case.

A lawyer who formally worked for the government is prohibited from representing a private client after they leave government service if the cases are in any way related. For example, if a lawyer served as the prosecuting attorney for the state against an individual for any crime, that lawyer cannot represent the accused party as a private attorney at a later date, for any case, after they have left government service. No past or future cases should impede a lawyer's ability to represent a client fairly and fully. Information about any case worked while under government service also needs to remain confidential, especially in a situation in which government information might aid a private client with their case. Any private client that has interests that conflict against the government they previously worked for is generally forbidden from representation by the attorney. However, if a firm hires a former government lawyer, the firm is permitted to screen that employee from taking part in a private case involving a client the employee may have a personal conflict of interest with.

J. Former Judge, Arbitrator, Mediator, or Other Third-Party Neutral

Lawyers who were once judges, arbitrators, mediators, or another third-party neutral for a dispute are, in general, prohibited from representing clients that have connections to any previous cases they worked as such. However, if there is written consent from all parties involved in the case and the client has full knowledge of past work performed by the lawyer, an exception can be made to this rule. Still, all information from previous employment that could help or hurt a client's case is required to be kept confidential. If the lawyer is part of a firm, the firm may also screen the attorney who may have a conflict of interest due to past work in the law field so that they can still represent the client without the lawyer taking part.

A lawyer is also prohibited from acting as a judge, **arbitrator** (an individual who is chosen as an impartial agent for a case to help resolve the dispute), mediator, or other third-party negotiator for any client they have represented or plan to represent. Because an arbitrator needs to be impartial, they would not be able to fully commit to one client's best interests. However, if the lawyer is only serving as a law clerk (someone who assists a judge with research and various legal work during a case), they can still represent a client in a related case if they first inform the judge and an agreement is made.

Domain V - Competence, Legal Malpractice, and Other Civil Liability

A. Maintaining Competence

A competent attorney is one who is qualified, either through training or experience, to represent a client's best interests in a case. This includes maintaining the level of professionalism established by the local jurisdiction throughout one's entire employment as an attorney, before, during, and after a case. Attorneys must adhere to a high standard to keep the profession honorable and trustworthy and to protect clients from being taken advantage of and forced to pay for services a lawyer may not have competently performed or that were outside of the attorney's abilities. To enter the legal profession, all attorneys should have at least a general understanding of the law and how law firms are organized; therefore, when an attorney agrees to represent a client, they are agreeing to use their training and experience to maintain this level of competence. This includes staying up to date on new laws that might help influence a case and, if necessary, completing additional education to stay abreast of how the law evolves over time, in addition to completing the standard educational and exam requirements. The most successful lawyers are able to consistently offer all the knowledge and expertise they have obtained in their field to help their clients succeed.

In addition to continuing education and keeping up with new regulations, a lawyer must maintain their competence by staying knowledgeable about new technologies and methods that can be used in the profession to offer additional assistance to a client. An attorney needs to ensure their practice never falls behind in terms of technological advances, as this would ultimately hinder their ability to do everything they can to fulfill their client's goals or give a possible advantage to their opponents. The attorney also needs to understand their client's opinions and ethical values, and the culture in general, to keep standards consistent with the times and provide those they represent with detailed explanations behind advisory actions.

B. Competence Necessary to Undertake Representation

In order for an attorney to be qualified to represent a client in a specific situation, they need to have at least a general understanding of the laws that will be involved and the practices to be carried out. A competent lawyer possesses the education, training, and experience relevant to a case. However, this does not mean that newly licensed lawyers are incompetent; if the client determines the attorney has studied enough and acquired the requisite skill set and knowledge to undertake a case, the attorney can still be considered competent for the job. Nevertheless, although a lawyer may not need extensive experience in the matter, their understanding and aptitude needs to be broad enough to fully accomplish the goals established in a lawyer-client contract. If a client is requesting services a lawyer does not feel they have the ability to complete, the lawyer should refrain from representing the client, especially in matters that involve specific knowledge of a particular area of law.

A lawyer is performing competently during a case if they are putting in the required time to fully research and investigate the situation using the ethical guidelines of their jurisdiction. Competent lawyers are also expected to thoroughly and correctly prepare all documentation required during a case. The lawyer needs to have a full understanding of the proper legal methods necessary to complete each task. Before representation, there should be a clear understanding and agreement between lawyer and

29

client that outlines the type and scope of the work the client desires. This way, both the lawyer and the client fully understand what needs to be accomplished and what steps must be taken to fulfill the established goals. If the attorney feels that a certain task in a client's request falls outside of their ability to competently represent the client, they may limit their scope of representation to include only the duties they have the most knowledge of and experience with.

C. Exercising Diligence and Care

A lawyer who exercises diligence and care when representing a client is one who performs an adequate amount of work to complete an established task or help a client win a case. Diligence is the attorney's ability to thoroughly understand the methods needed to complete the objectives and carry them out to the best of their knowledge and ability, making sure that all the possible solutions to a problem are examined and the best option is chosen. The attorney should never let personal matters or other obligations impede their ability to represent the client to the best of their abilities. Once the goals are established and agreed upon in the lawyer-client contract, the attorney needs to dedicate an adequate amount of time to understanding and completing the objectives. However, diligence in the law profession also includes realizing when an objective or task is taking an unnecessary amount of time or is being postponed from completion long enough to negatively affect the client's case. The diligent lawyer should know how to best allocate their time when working on a case that involves a large workload or multiple parties.

A lawyer should also use the proper care when working for a client. They should express an interest in helping the client to the best of their capabilities. This means maintaining consistent communication with the client and relaying any new information that could affect the outcome of a case. The client should also be knowledgeable of any type of lawyer-client contract formed between the parties and be aware of any circumstances that might break the contract and require new representation. The client should have a full understanding of the possible outcomes of their situation, and the lawyer who exercises care in a case will ensure their client understands why what is being done is important and relevant to their objectives. Exercising care means taking the time necessary to completely represent the client's best interests, making sure the client feels like they are receiving the best representation the attorney is able to offer.

D. Civil Liability to Client, Including Malpractice

When an individual becomes a client through an established and agreed-upon lawyer-client contract, the lawyer has a civil liability to the client. This means the attorney is responsible for fulfilling the contract to the best of their abilities or they'll risk being liable to civil action from the client for malpractice. The civil liability pertains to more than just winning cases for a client or completing the tasks assigned to them through the contract; it is a responsibility to perform duties to the best of the attorney's abilities. Losing a case in itself would not be considered a civil liability or result in malpractice as long as the attorney did everything in their power to adequately represent their client. Not all cases will be won, but every case still demands a certain amount of work and an upholding of jurisdictional and professional ethical codes.

Malpractice results when a lawyer does not uphold their agreement to a client or when they take an action that goes against the jurisdictional authority or code of ethics. Although, in general, any failure on

the attorney's part to perform adequate work in attempting to fulfill a client's requests could be considered malpractice if reasonably proven, malpractice most often occurs in a few specific instances. If a lawyer takes too long to complete an objective or procrastinates on work that needs to be done for a client, they are engaging in malpractice because they are not being diligent enough to represent their client's best interests. If the attorney commits routine errors in legal preparation or forgets to inform the client of key information related to their case, they are committing malpractice. Any failure in the attorney's duties to apply the law in the correct, ethical way to aid their client could result in malpractice. Also, if the lawyer does not gain the proper consent for a decision that only the client is allowed to make or if the lawyer goes against the client's desires, they are committing malpractice by not doing what is requested of them, breaking the lawyer-client contract.

E. Civil Liability to Nonclients

In general, an attorney does not have any liability to individuals with whom they have not first established a lawyer-client contract. The client and the attorney need to exchange information and come to an agreement about how the attorney can best help and represent the client before liabilities are created. However, an individual may still reveal confidential information to an attorney they do not end up hiring or forming a contract with. In these instances, the lawyer is still liable to keep this information confidential and refraining from using the information against the individual in any way to benefit another case or the attorney personally.

There are, however, a few instances when a lawyer's actions for a client affect other parties, creating civil liabilities for the attorney to nonclients. For example, if an attorney's work for a client indirectly causes the client's business partners to incur unnecessary loss or damage, the lawyer could be liable for any malpractice that may have caused the harm to the nonclients. Also, if the attorney represents a corporation or multiple clients who hold monetary interest in a case, the attorney may be liable for damages resulting from financial loss to those who were involved but not necessarily named in the contract. For example, if an attorney loses money for a corporation, they are liable to members of the board of directors who may have also lost money due to malpractice. There are also several instances when an attorney may be liable to their client's opposing party. This might happen if the attorney threatens or tries to influence the opposition in a way that makes them uncomfortable. Also, if the opposition believes the attorney committed illegal acts in an attempt to win a settlement for their own client or employed tactics that were unethical in order to cause damages to the opposing party, the lawyer would be subjected to civil liability from the nonclient.

F. Limiting Liability for Malpractice

If a lawyer is accused of malpractice, they could lose their ability to study law or, at the very least, have their reputation diminished. This is why some lawyers might want to take precautions before entering into a contract with a client to ensure the client does not make a malpractice claim against them. However, lawyers are generally not allowed to limit their liability for malpractice in a contract. For example, an attorney is not allowed to include specific clauses in a contract that prohibit the client from making a malpractice claim against the attorney. The attorney also is not allowed to forbid a client from making a malpractice claim as part of a settlement or to include in a settlement an agreement to retract a malpractice claim already made against the attorney. This rule extends to the attorney's former and current clients. A lawyer-client contract should never restrict the client's right to hold their attorney accountable for negligence or misconduct.

31

In addition to restricting the attorney from contractually prohibiting a client from making a malpractice claim, the attorney must also allow the client to find additional representation from another attorney before a misconduct claim is settled. Even if a client feels they do not need alternate representation, the lawyer needs to advise the client that they can and should seek a new attorney before any settlements are made regarding malpractice. A client who brings such a claim against a lawyer or firm has to know they have the opportunity and time to find an attorney who will help them in a case against a former or current attorney they believe has committed some form of malpractice. An independent attorney who does not work at the firm of the lawyer being accused of the malpractice should represent the client when the case is brought up. If the client was not given the opportunity to seek alternate representation, they risk being taken advantage of or agreeing to terms in a settlement that might be against the professional code of conduct for the practicing of law.

G. Malpractice Insurance and Risk Prevention

Depending on the settlement, a malpractice claim, if proven, can cause significant monetary damage to an attorney and their firm. This is why a lot of states mandate that a lawyer have malpractice insurance to help cover damages that may result from malpractice cases. If a lawyer is found guilty of malpractice, the insurance covers part or all of the damages the firm or attorney would personally have to pay. The insurance also ensures that the client is able to collect the full settlement from the malpractice claim, even if the lawyer or firm does not have the funds to pay the full amount. However, it is important for an attorney to choose the right type of insurance to make sure they are covered for any kind of settlement. Different types of insurance cover different types of firms and situations. Some types may only cover established firms or full-time attorneys. Other policies might have a higher deductible or a limit to the amount the insurance will pay out in a settlement. Some policies might assist with costs incurred while helping a client find independent representation when making a malpractice claim.

In addition to malpractice insurance, an attorney can use other risk prevention methods to mitigate their losses during a malpractice settlement. An attorney can choose a firm that specializes in malpractice claims to assist them with advice on preventive methods or even for representation during a case. Many law firms specialize in representing attorneys. Detailed documentation of work performed and how this work might pertain to reaching a client's objectives should also be kept in case an instance of malpractice is brought against an attorney. A lawyer is permitted to release even confidential information of a case if it is used in defense against a malpractice claim. The best way to prevent the risk of being charged with malpractice is to study and strictly follow the ethical guidelines laid out by the local jurisdiction. That way, if a claim is made against an attorney who has diligently followed the state's

guidelines for practicing law, they are able to prove that any malpractice claims brought against them are unwarranted and outside of the nature of the attorney and the firm.

Most Common Malpractice Claims

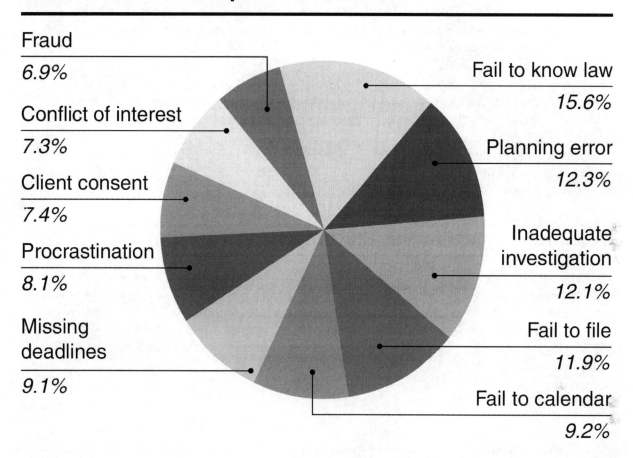

Fraud
6.9%

Conflict of interest
7.3%

Client consent
7.4%

Procrastination
8.1%

Missing deadlines
9.1%

Fail to know law
15.6%

Planning error
12.3%

Inadequate investigation
12.1%

Fail to file
11.9%

Fail to calendar
9.2%

Domain VI - Litigation and Other Forms of Advocacy

A. Meritorious Claims and Contentions

An attorney has a duty to do all they can within the bounds of the law to fully represent their client to the best of their abilities after a contract has been formed. However, there will be times when a client makes a claim or contention that goes beyond the scope of the law and the attorney's ability to fully achieve the client's objectives. An attorney is only obligated to accept cases that have potential to be won or completed within the bounds of what the attorney can legally do to help their client. If a client's objectives require an abuse of power, a manipulation of the law, or an outright unreasonable request, the attorney is permitted to limit the scope of their representation. However, the circumstances of a case are always liable to change through the passing of time and acquisition of new knowledge, so it is at the attorney's discretion to determine which of their potential client's claims and contentions are meritorious to peruse (meaning the most likely to be completed and paid for within a reasonable amount of time) and have the best chance at success.

A claim cannot be considered unmeritorious just because the client is unable to supply enough information about the situation or not enough evidence has been discovered to support their case. The attorney is responsible for learning as much as they can about the client's situation and how they can best represent them given their objectives. Even if a lawyer believes a client's case will result in a loss, this does not warrant enough cause to forgo representation. The attorney would need to prove the client's claims or contentions were fundamentally unethical or unable to be completed upon their presentation to the lawyer. This rule does not apply to an attorney who is court-ordered to represent a client in a specific case. However, even in all situations, the attorney would still need to act within the bounds of the ethical code.

B. Expediting Litigation

A lawyer is expected to perform diligent and careful work during a case to ensure the proper procedures are followed and the most useful evidence is found to support their client's dispute. However, spending too much time on tasks or not completing goals in a timely manner in order to further an objective could be considered malpractice if it negatively affects a client's chances of winning their case. The attorney has a responsibility to expedite litigation to the best of their abilities to settle disputes before they are dragged out for too long. Also, if a client is paying the attorney by the hour, spending unnecessary time on projects could be seen as an attempt to take advantage of the client by charging them excessively for things that could, and should, be expedited. Nevertheless, if the client is insisting that their attorney spend more time on litigation, the attorney must obey the request. Contracts might also contain specific dates for completing objectives, which should be followed by the attorney.

Litigations generally need to be handled in a timely matter and according to a client's requests; however, there are a few instances when a postponement may be acceptable. Certain personal obligations or family matters that an attorney is obligated to attend to would constitute an acceptable cause for not expediting litigation. Also, if the delay could be proven to benefit the client's situation, a postponement would be acceptable if agreed upon by the client. Excessive delays or postponements during a litigation could, however, become malpractice if not specifically requested by the party being represented. Additionally, an attorney should never forgo expediting litigation in order to delay responding to an opposing party's request for an appeal. All litigations should be handled in a timely

C. Candor to the Tribunal

An attorney is expected to use complete candor when addressing a tribunal for a case. This means they should never knowingly make false statements or refrain from correcting a false statement when presenting information to the court. Facts, not false information or ambiguous statements, should be used in prosecution and defense to support a case. Using false information to further a client's cause would be deceiving and could mislead the tribunal based on information the attorney knows is untrue. The attorney is also obligated to inform the tribunal if they know their client is planning to break the law or bring harm to another party. Also, during discussing between the attorney and the tribunal when the client is not present, the lawyer is expected to inform the tribunal of all the necessary facts in the case that could be used to make a decision in the matter, even if the facts may hurt the client's case. Refraining from telling the tribunal important, honest facts during a case is considered malpractice and goes against the standard ethical guidelines for attorneys as determined by the American Bar Association.

Candor to the tribunal extends to information given by the attorney's clients or witnesses who are used to support the case. The lawyer is responsible for ensuring that the facts of the case are always truthful and refraining from allowing their client to make false statements, even to win the case. If the lawyer finds out later that information provided to the tribunal from a client was false or misleading, it is their duty to inform the tribunal about the false information. The lawyer must also inform the tribunal of any information a witness used during litigation that is later realized to be false. Information used to further a case should always be true to avoid influencing the tribunal to make an unjust decision. Even if a client or witness demands that their lawyer use false evidence for a case, the lawyer is permitted to go against their client's wishes to keep their expected candor to the tribunal.

D. Fairness to Opposing Party and Counsel

Although the attorney is responsible for doing as much as they can to support their client, they are also expected to treat every case with fairness toward any opposing party or counsel. Fair competition means opposing parties should not go outside the bounds of the law in order to gain an unfair advantage. An attorney is forbidden from hiding or destroying evidence that could have a significant

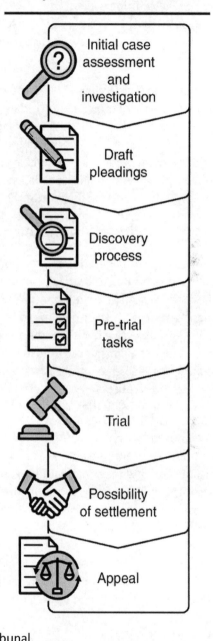

Steps Needed To Complete a General Case

- Initial case assessment and investigation
- Draft pleadings
- Discovery process
- Pre-trial tasks
- Trial
- Possibility of settlement
- Appeal

impact on the outcome of a case. Knowingly preventing evidence from being exposed in a case, whether harmful to a client or not, is considered unlawful and malpractice. An attorney is also not allowed to advise their employee or client to hide and prevent evidence from being obtained by another party or to encourage or bribe a client to engage in illegal activity or give false testimony to aid their case. Going against the wishes of the tribunal could be seen as taking advantage of a situation on unlawful grounds. The local jurisdictional authority determines the rules that should be followed for each case to ensure fairness to both parties.

The law grants attorneys the right to obtain evidence through lawful discovery. Opposing attorneys should not restrict this right by hiding or destroying key evidence that could determine the outcome of a case. This extends to misleading the opposition through false claims or hiding important documents and evidence. An attorney is permitted to interpret and present the evidence the way they see fit to best help the case, but any lies or twisting of facts used against the opposition obscures the tribunal's ability to make an informed decision. Fairness is the basis of the judicial system and is enforced by laws that govern how to best settle disputes according to the facts that can be obtained by both parties.

E. Impartiality and Decorum of the Tribunal

An attorney is obligated to remain honest and follow the rules set out by the local jurisdiction regarding ethical procedures to both the opposing party of a case and the tribunal who has influence over deciding the outcome. An attorney is not allowed to try and unlawfully sway a judge or juror in support of their client's case or for their own personal interests. The tribunal needs to remain impartial in order to deliver an objective decision regarding the outcome of a dispute. Any unfair influence in favor of one party would be considered unjust and contrary to the objectives of the tribunal. The decorum of the tribunal is created to ensure impartiality is maintained at all times during decision making. The attorney is expected to observe and participate in this decorum at all times by not embellishing arguments with untruths or abusing their influence over clients, judges, and jurors.

The impartiality and decorum of the tribunal also disallows the attorney from meeting with the tribunal without the client present, unless given permission by the client or required by the jurisdiction. This includes private meetings with judges or witnesses who might be used to influence the outcome of a case. The rule also gives the court the authority to preclude an attorney from meeting with a juror after a case has ended and the jury has been dismissed. Additionally, if a juror expresses that they do not wish to speak with the attorney after a case, the attorney is not allowed to pursue any type of discussion. A juror, whether active or potential, should never feel uncomfortable or in any way mistreated when speaking with an attorney, and the attorney is forbidden from other disrespectful conduct that seeks to disrupt a trial to prevent an unfavorable outcome. No outside influence apart from an argument using the facts and evidence of a case should be used to affect the decisions of the tribunal.

F. Trial Publicity

A certain amount of publicity is attached to every trial. Some trials may even cause a considerable amount of publicity, especially higher-profile criminal cases or cases involving well-known clients. An attorney who is participating in a case that is attracting publicity has a responsibility to the parties involved to limit the amount of information that is publicly exposed. In general, a lawyer needs to refrain from detailing any information about a case that could affect the outcome or give unfair advantage to one of the parties. However, not all information can or should be kept from the public. If an attorney is contacted for public comment about a case from the media or any other organization,

they are permitted to discuss certain aspects of the case, including what the dispute generally constitutes, any potential strategies being used in support of the client, and (when allowed by the jurisdiction) the details of the parties involved in the case. Any information already known and accessible by the public can also be discussed, including recent progress in the hearing or any progress to be taken. This information is considered important to ensuring the true facts of a case are known before any untruths can spread that might harm one of the parties involved.

Confidential information is generally restricted from being made available to the public through the attorney unless already done by another party or requested by the client. However, when public danger is involved or an attorney is requesting assistance in preventing unlawful or dangerous acts, the attorney is permitted to detail any relevant information to the public that could help keep them safe. This includes any personal information related to non-apprehended suspects or any law enforcement involved in the apprehension or protection of a suspect. Nevertheless, information given to the public in these circumstances must only be related to details that can help ensure the safety of the public or prevent illegal activity.

G. Lawyer as Witness

It is the attorney's job to use the testimonies and documents found or given by others in relation to a dispute to compile the necessary details to support their client. The lawyer is not responsible for providing evidence from events they were personally involved in and are specifically prohibited from giving testimony in a case in which they are already acting as a representative for one or more of the parties involved. This rule ensures that there is no conflict of interest between a client and the information the attorney might provide during testimony. It also keeps the attorney from influencing the case as a witness, giving unjust advantage to their client or opponent. The lawyer might also use themselves as a witness in order to try and confuse the jurors or opposition, which would be an unethical abuse of an attorney's power to influence a tribunal.

There are, however, several instances in which a lawyer is permitted to act as a witness. If the information provided while giving testimony was related to a simple matter of fact that is not being contested, the lawyer may testify. If the lawyer is giving testimony about the type and scope of work they performed for a client, the testimony would also be permitted. Even if a lawyer's testimony is detrimental to the outcome of a case, the attorney still needs to be released from representing any of the clients involved before they can act as a witness. However, in situations in which dismissing the lawyer would cause a significant personal hardship for the client involved and evidence can be supplied to prove the potential hardship, the lawyer may be permitted to act both as a witness and an attorney for the client if allowed by the jurisdiction. An attorney is permitted, however, to act as a witness in a case in which they are not acting as an active lawyer, even including cases taken by attorneys at their firm.

Domain VII - Transactions and Communications with Persons Other Than Clients

A. Truthfulness in Statements to Others

When discussing a client or case, a lawyer has a duty to never provide or endorse false information about the situation to anyone, including those who are not involved. The lawyer must also refrain from giving misleading and untrue information about the law in general or providing information that could be used to commit a crime. The attorney is a representative of their jurisdiction and must act within the jurisdiction's ethical guidelines when working as such and providing individuals with information related to the law. This means lawyers must use their full knowledge of the law and avoid giving individuals half-truths or ambiguous statements that could cause legal trouble for a third party if used incorrectly. Any opinions about a case or an interpretation of the law should be disclaimed as such, and precedence should be given to supplying individuals with only true facts when available, whether they are a client of the attorney or not.

Although an attorney is expected to maintain truthfulness in their statements to others, they are not required to release all the factual information they might know about a case to a third party or their opposition. An attorney may want to keep certain information confidential in order to aid their client and not give out evidence that could hurt their case. Information is only required to be disclosed by the attorney if it relates to the committing of a crime. If a client is asking for information about how to commit a crime, the lawyer is allowed to forgo representation and may be required to disclose any information to the jurisdiction to stop the crime from being committed. The lawyer is forbidden from aiding any party in committing crimes and may face prosecution for assisting a criminal if information relating to the incident is not disclosed.

B. Communications with Represented Persons

When a lawyer agrees to represent a client in a given case, they are no longer allowed to discuss the matters of the case to any other party that might be represented by a different attorney involved in the dispute, unless they first obtain the permission to do so by the other attorney. This rule is used to prevent lawyers from taking advantage of other parties in a case or creating a conflict of interest between the attorney and the client they chose to represent. Even if the attorney is first asked for information by the other party, they must refrain from discussing the case unless the other party's attorney agrees to the discussion before it takes place. If the attorney finds out later that the person they spoke with was someone involved in the case and is represented by another attorney, they must discontinue all communication with the person and refrain from detailing any more information about the case. In an instance in which an attorney might represent a number of individuals, such as when representing a corporation, communication about the case with any party of the organization who regularly comes into contact with their attorney is prohibited by those who do not directly represent the organization involved.

An attorney is still permitted to discuss any details that are irrelevant to the case or representation to any party they choose. An attorney can also provide counsel or discuss law-related issues with a person who is already represented by another attorney as long as the attorney giving the information is not involved in the case at all. As for discussion between clients, these communication rules only apply to

38

lawyers who are representing separate parties in a case; two opposing clients or two clients with different representation are permitted to discuss matters related to the legal situation at their own discretion if they desire.

C. Communications with Unrepresented Persons

Unrepresented persons constitute individuals or parties that do not already have legal representation for a dispute. When an unrepresented person seeks the assistance or advice of an attorney, they are requesting consultation and possible council. An attorney is permitted to provide consultation to unrepresented persons as long as they are not related in any way to a case the attorney is already involved with. If the unrepresented person is seeking counsel related to a case the attorney is already taking part in, the attorney is forbidden from giving the individual information related to the case or providing any advice outside of suggesting the party find their own representation. An attorney who agrees to represent a client for a case has a responsibility to the client to not give any information that might go against the client's wishes or harm their chances of success in their case; this is why a lawyer must be very particular about who they speak with concerning matters relating to their cases.

A misunderstanding can sometimes ensue if an unrepresented person is turned down or not permitted to speak with an attorney without explanation. In these situations, the attorney is allowed to disclose who they represent and why this representation might cause a conflict of interest if discussed with the unrepresented person. The lawyer is also permitted to discuss negotiations with an unpresented person on behalf of their client if given permission. However, anytime an attorney is approached by an unrepresented person for advice on matters related to a case the attorney is taking part in, the attorney must clearly state that they are representing a client who may have adverse objectives in relation to the unrepresented person and that the attorney's main priority is supporting their client in the case and no other involved party.

D. Respect for Rights of Third Persons

An attorney's first priority in a case is their client. The lawyer is expected to perform the tasks and complete the objectives agreed upon in the lawyer-client relationship to help the client's case. This means the lawyer has ultimate responsibility for protecting their client's information from being used against them in a dispute. However, this does not mean a lawyer has no responsibilities or duties toward the opposition and those they are not representing. An attorney should show basic respect to all individuals they speak with and come into contact with while practicing the law. Lawyers are not permitted to use their time or efforts on a case strictly to humiliate, discomfort, or cause unnecessary harm to third persons. All actions should be taken to further a client's cause but in a manner that is conscious of how they might unnecessarily affect the other parties involved. Any attempt made by a lawyer to personally harm or cause discomfort to a third party that could not be justifiably proven to help their client is considered malpractice and is subject to punishment by the jurisdiction.

Respect for the rights of third persons includes realizing when a third party or opposing party has made a mistake and exposed evidence or documents they might not have wanted exposed. In this case, the lawyer needs to use their best judgment regarding how the evidence was obtained, and if the information was acquired in a way that could be considered fraudulent or as a result of a mistake, the lawyer is responsible for informing the person they obtained the information from. For example, if a document is known to have been accidently forwarded or leaked in a way that exposes the information to the opposing attorney, the attorney needs to notify the person who sent the information and inform

them that they have released possibly dangerous information. Even if the information could benefit their client, the method of obtaining the information needs to be disclosed to keep the case fair. All attorneys should respect the ethical process of fair competition during a case in order to uphold the standards set by the jurisdiction that keep the practice of law respectable and trustworthy.

Domain VIII - Different Roles of the Lawyer

A. Lawyer as Advisor

One of the most important roles of the attorney is acting as an advisor for those who are seeking legal consultation. A client represented by the attorney expects to receive truthful, beneficial law advice as it relates to their situation to help complete their objectives or win a case. However, in being honest, the lawyer may have to give advice the client may not want to hear. The lawyer needs to always keep a professional manner when presenting any type of information in order to avoid making a client feel like the attorney is unempathetic to their situation. Lawyers should also avoid giving advice in technical terms a client might not be able to fully understand. Any information that may be beneficial to a client requesting advice should be given in a clear, professional way so the client can better understand the case as a whole.

Even after a lawyer-client relationship has been formed, an attorney is not required to give legal advice to parties unless first asked. However, after forming the relationship, if the attorney believes the client is at risk of performing an action that might negatively affect their case, the attorney can advise the client on why their action may cause a negative outcome and suggest an alternative, even when not first asked by the client. There is no responsibility, however, for a lawyer to do research and give counsel to a client on matters the client may not want consultation on. Advice should also always be related to the law; the attorney should avoid attempting to offer advice on matters that might be outside of their expertise. A lawyer in these situations would be required to suggest the client visit a different type of professional when asked for advice about anything other than legal matters.

B. Lawyer as Evaluator

A lawyer is acting as an evaluator when they inspect evidence and documentation related to a case in order to present this information to their client or another party to further their client's objectives. A lawyer is constantly evaluating information to determine the best course of action to take during representation. Basic evaluation can be performed with or without the expressed desire of the client as long as it is used to help the lawyer, or even a third party, better understand the client's legal situation. A lawyer is permitted to evaluate a third party as well if they believe it will be beneficial to achieving the goals set out by an established agreement with their client. The lawyer can also provide the client's legal details to third parties, such as the government, if required, or when the evaluation will cause no harm to the client. However, if the disclosing of information to a third party during an evaluation could have any effect on the client's situation, the attorney must detail any potential danger to the client and receive expressed consent to continue the evaluation.

Evaluation is done in order to ensure that no important details in a case are left undiscovered and to avoid using information that could be false. Thorough evaluation involves not only collecting data but also interpreting the data in a way that can be used to positively affect a case. Evaluation includes organizing relevant information in a way that can be understood and accessed easily when needed. When acting as an evaluator, the successful lawyer will combine their knowledge of the law with the ability to research and find evidence related to a client's case to fulfill the obligations of their lawyer-client contract.

41

C. Lawyer as Negotiator

The role of the negotiator for a lawyer requires an ability to both reach an outcome in a case that is beneficial to their client and to ensure they are acting in a fair and ethical way toward other involved parties. Negotiating is more than just getting the best deal for the client. The lawyer must always ensure they are acting within the bounds of the law and the rules of their jurisdiction when influencing outcomes during negotiations. The lawyer should never seek to take advantage of the power they might hold over jurors, judges, or an opposing party with less knowledge of the law. All negotiations should be made with fairness as the ultimate goal, based on the facts of the case. Negotiations should, of course, still be made with the client's best interests in mind, but these interests should never be used as justification for unethical or unlawful behavior.

To be a strong negotiator, the lawyer needs to first have a thorough understanding of the laws pertaining to their client's situation and how these laws can be used to benefit the client when it comes time to settle a dispute. The successful negotiator is one who can persuade their audience in favor of their client using the facts of the case and adroit interpretations of the law. The lawyer must also keep in mind that, in addition to the best interests of their clients, they are always representing their jurisdiction and the propriety of the law. This is why the lawyer, as a negotiator, must balance these respective interests to complete their client's goals while emphasizing fairness and justice in every legal proceeding.

D. Lawyer as Arbitrator, Mediator, or Other Third-Party Neutral

Because a lawyer has considerable knowledge about the law and how cases are settled, they are often assigned to resolve disputes between parties rather than act as a client's representative. A lawyer is permitted to serve as an arbitrator, mediator, or other third-party neutral for a case in which they are not already representing a client. The role of arbitrator consists of independently settling disputes between opposing parties. A mediator acts as a professional assigned to help two parties come to an agreement based on the facts of the case and the rules of the law. Third-party neutral assignments consist of any other position or duty an attorney might be asked to perform when acting as an independent party that objectively hears the arguments put forth by opposing parties in a dispute and examining the evidence of the case to help determine a fair outcome that will be agreeable to both parties.

When a lawyer is serving as a representative of the law to help settle disputes in a case, they are subjected to the rules that govern arbitrators in their jurisdiction. The American Bar Association has published rules that strictly pertain to neutral parties acting as arbitrator, mediator, or other third-party neutral. The individual who steps outside of their role as an attorney should familiarize themselves with and follow the ethical rules that pertain to whatever position they decide to take. A lawyer also needs to make it clearly apparent to all parties involved in a dispute that they are not acting as anyone's attorney but are instead taking the position of the third party assigned to help settle the dispute. An attorney is forbidden to give consultation or any information that could be used as an unfair advantage for one of the parties and should be aware of any conflicts of interest that might exist between one of the parties involved and their role as an arbitrator. Even if one or more of the people involved in the dispute are

unrepresented, the attorney must clearly state that they are only acting as an arbitrator, mediator, or third-party neutral and cannot act in any way as a representative for the party.

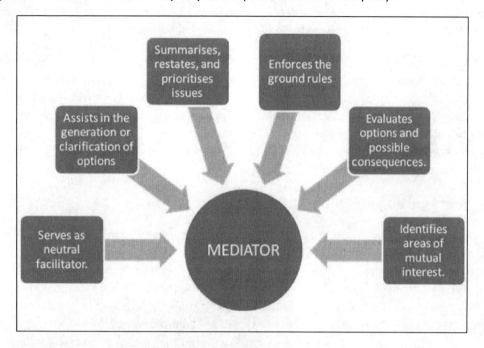

E. Prosecutors and Other Government Lawyers

Prosecutors are attorneys who serve in criminal cases that make claims against a defendant. When someone commits a crime, the prosecuting attorney is the lawyer assigned to make a case against the suspect. Most prosecutors work for the government, as it is usually the state or jurisdiction that brings charges against individuals based on violations of their law. Prosecutors are employed by the government and assigned criminal cases in which they must represent the position of the state or federal government. This means the client of the prosecutor is the government, and the lawyer would be subjected to the same rules regarding representation, including rules of confidentiality, the responsibility to expedite litigation, and the obligation to do all they can within the law to prosecute the suspected criminal using the facts and evidence of the case. However, depending on the jurisdiction, a prosecuting attorney or other government lawyer may be subjected to different disclosure rules that are more open than those mandated to private attorneys. A government attorney may be required to disclose any evidence or information that could be used by the accused to prove their innocence or to lessen the punishment for the crimes. This is because the government attorney is first responsible to ensure that justice and fairness are preserved in government trials to avoid the prosecution of an innocent party rather than attempting to complete objectives that only support a client's case and not disclosing information that could go against their client's case.

F. Lawyer Appearing in Nonadjudicative Proceeding

A lawyer may be asked to take part in a number of cases involving nonadjudicative proceedings. A nonadjudicative proceeding is a meeting between opposing parties overseen by a mediator rather than an arbitrator. This means the parties are in charge of determining the outcome of the case rather than a neutral third party. However, an attorney is still expected to adhere to the same rules and regulations pertaining to their responsibility to their client and to the ethical guidelines of the jurisdiction. This

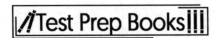

means they must keep client information confidential and still act in a way that will best benefit their client's situation within the limits of the law. They should also be confident enough to adequately negotiate and make decisions that will benefit their client while keeping in mind the situation of the other party and what conditions they might desire before a settlement can be made.

Sometimes, a lawyer may participate in a non-adjudicative meeting when they are not currently representing a client, such as meetings with a government or other legislative agency. It is the attorney's responsibility to disclose to all parties involved in a nonadjudicative proceeding whether they are there to represent a client or not. The motives of all attorneys attending such a proceeding should be made clear to the tribunal and toward all those involved. Nevertheless, attorneys attending a nonadjudicative proceeding are expected to show the same respect and follow the same guidelines as they do when attending court hearings in which adjudicative proceedings are involved.

G. Lawyer Representing an Entity or Other Organization

An entity or organization is any group, corporation, or other body acting together to achieve common objectives in a case. This is in contrast to working with individual clients; the lawyer would be responsible for representing the interests of the group as a whole rather than specific, singular agendas. Corporations also can be involved in their own cases even though they are not technically human individuals. However, when representing an entity or organization, an attorney still needs to be able to communicate with someone in order to come to agreements and to defer decisions to. Large entities and organizations need to assign individuals who are designated to represent them and who will be in charge of communicating with the attorney and deciding on the terms of the lawyer-client contract.

When representing more than one person, it is possible that conflicts or differences of opinion will arise between members of the entity or organization. In general, the organization needs to have a common objective in opposition to another party in order to receive full representation by an attorney. Conflicts of interest between individuals in the same party could negate the lawyer-client relationship if the attorney is forced to choose sides. However, if one or more of the members of the entity or organization act or disclose information in a way that the attorney reasonably believes goes against or hurts the case of the organization as originally determined before the relationship was formed, the lawyer is entitled to take the steps they feel are necessary to act in the best interests of the entity or organization, even if they go against one of the members of the entity or organization's wishes.

Domain IX - Safekeeping Funds and Other Property

A. Establishing and Maintaining Client Trust Accounts

Attorneys often receive funds from clients to pay for services, court filings, and other expenses. When funds are paid upfront, they are referred to as retainers. A general retainer is a fee paid by the client to reserve the attorney's time should the need arise. This type of retainer is not used towards the payment of services. An advance payment retainer is a prepayment for services. The client pays in advance for the attorney's work. Both a general retainer and an advance payment retainer are paid directly to the attorney.

There is a third type of retainer—a security retainer—that is not paid directly to the attorney. A security retainer is monies paid upfront by the client to cover the attorney's fees and other expenses. Security retainers are a way of ensuring that the attorney will be paid for services rendered, regardless of the outcome of the case. This can be particularly important in financial cases, such as bankruptcies, but it can sometimes become an issue in cases where the client is dissatisfied with the outcome of the case. The security retainer monies are placed into a trust account and paid to the attorney as services are rendered and expenses are incurred in serving the client.

The trust account must also be safeguarded. The authorized signatory must be a legally licensed attorney in the practice or a person under the supervision of the attorney. All receipts for deposits must be detailed and maintained, and withdrawals from the account must be made to a named person or by electronic funds transfer. Payments cannot be made out in cash. Any funds remaining in the account at the conclusion of the case or upon the termination of the attorney-client relationship must be promptly returned to the client.

Because security retainer fees are not paid directly to the attorney, a client trust account must be established. The trust account must be created within the state where the attorney's practice is located unless otherwise agreed to by the client, such as in the case where the client lives in a neighboring state or jurisdiction. Statutes do not require that the trust account be held at a bank. However, the account must clearly indicate that the funds within belong to a person other than the attorney, and the attorney cannot in any way profit from the account. Any interest earned on the account, for example, belongs to the client.

In many cases, funds deposited on retainer are not sufficient to earn significant interest, either because they are of an insufficient amount or are held for an insufficient amount of time. In these cases, many states require that funds be deposited into an Interest on Lawyer Trust Account (IOLTA). These accounts pool client monies into amounts great enough to earn interest. The interest earned from an IOLTA must be used for the public good, such as providing legal services to the poor.

The attorney may not at any time commingle personal or business funds with the client's trust account funds. Laws against the commingling of funds help to protect client monies from collection by the attorney's creditors. They also ensure that attorneys cannot "hide" their own money within client trust accounts. The only exception to the commingling rules allows for attorneys to deposit their own funds into trust accounts to cover any fees or bank changes associated with the account. Amounts are limited to only enough money to cover such fees.

Attorneys must also promptly withdraw undisputed, earned payments from the trust account. Leaving earned monies in the account for long periods of time could constitute commingling. For example, if a client has paid money as a security retainer, and the attorney has earned some of that money through hourly billing, the attorney must withdraw the earned monies promptly upon billing and agreement by the client. If the attorney leaves the earned monies in the account, the account is no longer solely owned by the client but now also contains monies owned by the attorney, which constitutes commingling.

If there are disputed fees, however, the attorney must deposit those monies in a separate, joint account belonging to both the attorney and the client. The funds must remain in that account until the dispute is resolved, and then the funds should be dispersed accordingly. For example, Client A has paid a $10,000 security retainer with the understanding that Attorney B will use these funds to pay for court costs, expenses, and to cover the attorney's $300 per hour fee. Attorney B worked on the client's case for a total of twenty hours and paid $1,000 in court costs. Attorney B also hired an expert to write a statement on behalf of the client; this expert charged a fee of $2,000. At the conclusion of the case, the attorney returns the remaining $1,000 to the client. The client, however, is unhappy with the outcome of the case and disputes the attorney's rate of $300 per hour. The client claims that the attorney is only entitled to $200 per hour. Attorney B must put the disputed $2,000 (the $100 per hour difference for twenty hours) into a joint account until the dispute is resolved. The attorney is also required to suggest means for resolving the dispute, such as arbitration.

Attorneys must maintain detailed records of all trust accounts, including receipts for all deposits and withdrawals and records of wire transfers and other disbursements. These records must be maintained for at least five years after the termination of the attorney-client relationship.

B. Safekeeping Funds and Other Property of Clients

The use of trust accounts helps to protect client funds from misuse. Because the monies are clearly identified as belonging to the client, the attorney's creditors and other parties cannot seize the funds as payment for the attorney's debts. The attorney also cannot use the client's accounts to conceal their own monies from creditors or debt collectors or for other nefarious purposes. The client's monies are protected and can only be disbursed by agreement between the client and the attorney.

Attorneys must keep adequate records of all monies held on behalf of their clients. Written ledgers must be kept for all accounts that indicate the name of the client; the date, amount, and source of each deposit of funds; the date, amount, and payee of any disbursements made from the account; and the current balance in the account. Records should also include all bank statements, receipts, invoices, and canceled checks applicable to the account.

Similarly, attorneys must also protect any property belonging to the client that is left in the attorney's care. Attorneys are sometimes required to hold property that is of importance in any given case. For example, if an attorney is representing a client in a divorce, and there is a dispute over an expensive engagement ring, the judge may require that the attorney take possession of the ring pending the outcome of the case. Other types of cases in which attorneys may also hold property could include product liability cases regarding a defective product or documents in real estate or business cases. Attorneys are required to have a means of safeguarding the client's property pending the resolution of the case.

There are several requirements involved when an attorney takes possession of a client's property. First, the attorney must clearly identify and label the property, such as with a detailed description of the item, the client's name, and the case identifier. The attorney must then place the item in a safe, a safety deposit box, or other suitable secure location. The attorney must also notify any interested third parties that the item is in the attorney's possession. Some states require this notification within a set number of days. For example, the State of California requires that all parties be notified of the receipt of property within fourteen days. Upon the resolution of the case, the property must be promptly delivered to the appropriate party. For example, in the divorce and engagement ring case, the judge will determine who should receive the ring, and, upon that decision, the attorney must provide the ring to the appropriate party.

Finally, the attorney is required to keep complete written records of the property. These records must include a listing of the item, the person whom the attorney is holding the property for, the date of receipt of the item, and the date the property was distributed and to whom. Attorneys must maintain these records for at least five years after the termination of representation and must make these records available to the client upon request. The attorney is also required to make these records available in the event of an audit.

C. Safekeeping Funds and Other Property of Third Persons

Some occasions require an attorney to hold for safekeeping funds, assets, or other property that potentially belongs to a third party. The American Bar Association's Rule 1.15 specifically says that attorneys "should hold property of others with the care required of a professional fiduciary." This most often translates into maintaining a safe deposit box to hold securities, documents, and other property. If the property is too large to keep in a safe deposit box, a safe or other secure location may be maintained. Any property belonging to third parties must be held separate from the attorney's property, including keeping any monies in a separate trust account as the attorney must do with clients' money. Attorneys are not permitted to access or use the property for their own purposes. In addition, attorneys are required to protect the third-party property from interference by the client.

Safekeeping property or funds belonging to third parties most often occurs in situations where a third party has a lien against the client's money or property. There are several ways that liens are applied to a client's money or property, including legal statutes, court orders, or by agreements between the parties. For example, if there is still money owed on that expensive engagement ring, the creditor may serve the attorney with a notice prohibiting the attorney from relinquishing the ring pending the outcome of a judgment or bankruptcy proceeding to resolve the debt. Liens or interests in the financial outcome of litigation can also include situations such as paying medical service providers in a personal injury or accident case or paying debts such as past due child support from any judgment received.

When these situations arise, attorneys are not permitted to disburse funds or property but are instead required to safeguard the monies or property pending the resolution of the case, judgment, or dispute.

There may also arise situations in which the client and the third party have a dispute over the allocation of funds or property. Attorneys are not expected to mediate and resolve these disputes. However, in the event a dispute cannot be settled by the parties, the attorney may need to file a motion with the court to have the issue resolved.

D. Disputed Claims

Disputed claims can come in many forms. An attorney holding escrow money in a failed real estate transaction, for example, may find that both the seller and the potential buyer claim rights to the escrow funds. The potential buyer believes the funds to be theirs because they initially placed the monies into the escrow account. The seller may believe the funds belong to them if the buyer has violated the purchase contract. In this case, the attorney may not arbitrarily disburse funds to whomever they choose. Either the parties must resolve the dispute themselves, or the attorney may have to file a motion and ask the court to settle the matter. The attorney is responsible for holding the funds or property in safekeeping until the resolution of the dispute. Once the dispute is resolved, the attorney must promptly disburse the funds or property according to the agreement of the parties or the decision of the court.

Attorneys may also find themselves in dispute with their clients over retainer fees that were paid into the client's trust account, particularly when the outcome of the case is not to the client's liking. The client may not want to pay the attorney's fees or may dispute the payment of fees to the court or expert witnesses. The attorney should maintain detailed documentation of all fees billed to the client that are paid from the client's trust account. One option is for the attorney to require the client's signed approval for each disbursement from the account, such as having the client approve and sign all billing statements, requests for expert witnesses, and payments for court costs. This can be cumbersome at times, but it may help the attorney avoid disputes over costs and fees in the future since the client would have approved every withdrawal.

Sometimes disputes over funds may arise when a third party pays an attorney's retainer on behalf of the client. This can occur in criminal cases where the client has been arrested, and the client's family or other third party pays for the attorney's fees. Upon resolution of the case or termination of the attorney-client relationship, the third party may then seek a refund of any remaining fees they paid on behalf of the client. The attorney can find themselves caught between the party who paid the fees and the party whom the attorney actually represents. The best way to avoid this type of dispute is to make it clear to the third party that the funds are being paid on behalf of the client and are going to be considered a gift to the client. Thus, any refund of fees will be made to the client. Similarly, an agreement can be drawn up and signed by both parties indicating who should receive the refund of any remaining fees. Having a written agreement from the outset can help attorneys avoid disputes later on.

On occasion, attorneys may have unclaimed funds remaining in a trust account. This most often happens when the owner of the funds, be it a client or a third party, cannot be located. The attorney must make a reasonable effort to locate the owner of the funds, including calling all known phone numbers and mailing notifications to the party's last known address. If all efforts to contact the party have failed, the attorney must hold the funds in the trust account for at least three years, at which time the property is considered abandoned. The attorney can then look to the state statutes for how abandoned property should be handled and proceed accordingly. Regardless of status, the attorney is still required to maintain trust account records for at least five years after the resolution of the case and/or the termination of the attorney-client relationship.

Domain X - Communications About Legal Services

A. Advertising and Other Public Communications About Legal Services

Attorneys use many forms of advertising to attract new clients, from websites and online ads to television commercials, newspapers, billboards, and direct mail campaigns. Prior to 1976, attorneys were not permitted to advertise because the government believed that the average person was not well-versed enough in the law and legal matters to make educated determinations and decisions regarding legal representation. In 1977, the Supreme Court heard the case of *Bates v. State Bar of Arizona* and determined that total suppression of advertising was an interference with attorneys' First Amendment rights. However, the Court did determine that advertising by attorneys could be regulated due to the overall lack of legal understanding among the general public. As a result, all forms of advertising in the legal profession must adhere to strict standards and rules so as to not mislead or deliberately misinform clients. Attorneys must not in any way misrepresent themselves or their firm in their advertising.

There are 25 categories of information that attorneys are permitted to advertise:

1. Name, address, and telephone number of attorneys	14. Foreign languages
2. Fields of law practiced by the firm	15. Bank references
3. Date and place of birth of each attorney	16. Names of regular clients (with written permission from the client)
4. State and federal bar admissions and dates for each attorney	17. Availability of any prepaid legal plans
5. Schools attended and degrees earned by each attorney	18. Whether the firm accepts credit cards
6. Public or quasi-public offices held by attorneys in the firm	19. Office and phone answering hours
7. Military service	20. Initial consultation fees
8. Legal articles written by attorneys in the firm	21. Written fee schedules
9. Legal teaching positions held by firm attorneys	22. Contingent fee rates
10. Memberships in bar associations and committees and offices held	23. The range of fees for services
11. Memberships in legal fraternities or societies	24. The lawyers' hourly rates
12. Technical and professional licenses	25. The firm's fixed fees
13. Memberships in technical and professional societies	

49

While the information provided in these categories is protected by the First Amendment, attorneys must still take care that the information they include is true and accurate and is not in any way dubious or misleading.

Misrepresentation can be in the form of lawyers portraying themselves as something they are not, such as having certain skills, education, or experience that they do not possess. For example, an attorney may include information in a television advertisement that their firm won a multi-million dollar award on behalf of clients in a class action lawsuit. However, the attorney was not part of the firm when that lawsuit was won and, therefore, did not have any direct involvement in the case. This ad would be misleading to clients because it leads them to believe that the attorney has experience that the attorney does not actually have. This constitutes a misrepresentation of the attorney's experience.

Misrepresentation also includes the omission of relevant information, such as necessary facts that may affect the meaning or validity of the advertisement. Statements in advertising may be technically true while still being misleading if key facts or relevant information is omitted. For example, an attorney may advertise that they attended Harvard School of Law, which may be technically true but may also omit the key fact that they were expelled from the school before graduating. This would constitute a misleading advertisement about the attorney's relevant education because it leads potential clients to believe the attorney graduated from Harvard when that is not true.

Attorneys must also take care to manage client expectations based on advertisements. Their advertisements must not suggest to potential clients that their case will have the same outcome as past cases if they use a particular attorney. These types of advertisements occur frequently in personal injury cases where attorneys advertise huge settlements on past cases without noting that past performance is not a guarantee of future performance. Each case is different and dependent on the specific facts, details, and circumstances of that case and cannot be used as an accurate predictor of any future case. Advertisements must not lead clients to unfair expectations based on these past cases. These types of problems in advertising can often be avoided simply by including suitable disclaimers.

Attorneys are permitted to advertise their fees if such advertising includes true and accurate information and does not omit any necessary or relevant details. For example, an attorney can advertise that they handle divorce cases for a set fee. However, this could be misleading if the advertisement does not disclose that the attorney's fee does not include any court costs, filing fees, mandated parenting classes, or required moderation costs. The attorney's advertisement could potentially lead clients to believe they could get a divorce for the attorney's set fee when in reality, the costs could be much higher. The problem can be avoided by including a disclaimer that the attorney's set fee does not include court costs and fees.

Attorneys also must not compare themselves or their firm to other attorneys or firms without presenting reasonable, measurable evidence that supports the comparison. For example, an attorney cannot advertise that their firm is the most successful in the area or that they represent the most clients without some type of substantiated evidence that supports this claim. The attorney or firm can, however, use evidence from independent third parties in their advertising, so long as it is valid and clearly expressed. For example, claiming that ABC Law Firm was "voted the best in Jackson County in 2022" could be used in an advertisement so long as the source of this poll or survey is included: "ABC Law Firm was voted the best in Jackson County in 2022 according to New Jackson Now magazine."

It is important to note that firm names, professional designations, and letterheads are all subject to the same rules and guidelines as advertising. Including the names of current or former partners in the firm name is permissible so long as those people are or were active members of the firm. Firms may not include attorneys' names who have never had an affiliation with the firm. Firm names must also not suggest a connection with any government agency or charitable service organization. Care must be taken if a firm wishes to use a geographic designation so as to not mislead the public that the firm is affiliated with the city, town, county, or other governmental agency. Including a statement that the firm is not affiliated with any government or charitable organization may help avoid any misrepresentation. Better still would be to avoid firm names that may cause confusion.

Website addresses, trade names, and social media usernames must also accurately represent the firm and cannot be misleading in any way. Using a web address that suggests a connection to a government entity or other agency in authority is misleading and could be a violation of advertising rules.

All advertising, be it for a single attorney or a legal firm, must include the name of at least one attorney who is responsible for the contents of the advertisement. Additionally, a copy of the advertisement must be retained for at least two years, including information on when and where the advertisement was displayed, broadcast, or published.

B. Solicitation—Direct Contact with Prospective Clients

In addition to mass marketing, there are regulations around the direct solicitation of clients, as well. Solicitation is defined as direct contact with a specific person to address what the attorney knows or is reasonably expected to know about their specific legal needs. It is different from mass advertising because it targets the particular legal needs of a certain person as opposed to the general public.

Solicitation is limited when the attorney's primary purpose for the solicitation is employment or monetary gain. These limitations are predominantly around live, person-to-person contact, which means contact in real time, either in person, via phone, or by video chat. The limitations are based on the idea that real time contact does not allow the potential client to fully process the information and make a reflective, informed decision. Instead, they may feel pressured to respond immediately based on the urgency of their legal need and the potential persuasive techniques, undue influence, or even perceived intimidation by the attorney; thus, potential clients may feel pressured to make decisions based on in-the-moment emotions rather than being able consider the information and adequately compare alternatives.

There are some notable exceptions to the live contact rule. Attorneys are permitted to engage in live communication with other attorneys, people the attorney has a close familial or personal relationship with, people the attorney has a close business or professional relationship with, and former clients. Additionally, exceptions are provided for contact with people who routinely seek legal services for business purposes. These situations are excluded because attorneys are less likely to overreach or exert undue influence in these situations.

When soliciting business from potential clients, attorneys can avoid this type of negative or overwhelming influence by using other forms of communication, such as emails or text messages. Clients can easily disregard these types of communications and not feel pressured to respond immediately. Additionally, communicating with potential clients in writing protects both the client and the attorney from any confusion that may arise from real time live conversations. The contents of

written communications cannot be easily disputed. Attorneys can take care with the information they present to ensure its accuracy, and clients can take care to read and fully understand the information before making any type of decision or determination based on it.

Any type of direct communication is prohibited if it contains language that could be considered coercion or harassment, and communication is prohibited if the recipient has expressed a desire not to be contacted by the attorney. Solicitations are also prohibited when the potential client's mental ability or emotional state may make their judgment questionable, such as contacting grieving parents immediately after the death of their child.

C. Group Legal Services

Attorneys are allowed to approach groups that might be interested in legal representation or prepaid legal services, so long as those groups are not owned or managed by the law firm. For example, a local union might want to provide legal services to its members at a reduced group rate. This type of arrangement can include offers of prepaid legal services extended to the group and its members or subscriptions to a legal services plan being offered by the attorney or their law firm. This is not an offer of specific legal services extended to an individual in need of those services and thus does not violate the rules around individual solicitation. Instead, the attorney would be offering services to the group via a leader who may be seeking a service provider for the group.

The attorney must only approach the leader of the group or a group representative, such as the president of an organization or charter or a union representative with the authority to act on behalf of the union. The attorney may not contact individual members directly to solicit such an arrangement, and the offer of services cannot be tailored to nor directed toward any particular individual known to need legal services. For example, an attorney cannot approach an organization with an offer of legal services to vehicle accident victims because one of the group's members was recently injured in a car accident.

Once a legal services plan is established with the group's leader, the group may use live, person-to-person contact with the individual members to explain the arrangement and sign them up for the plan. The attorney offering the services may not participate in this individual contact. Solicitation can only be done by the group leader and their designees.

For example, Attorney A approaches the head of ABCD Labor Union with an offer of a prepaid legal services subscription plan for the union members. The union head will decide whether this is something that should be offered to the group. If so, the head will discuss and finalize the plan details with the attorney. The union leader or their designees will then solicit participation in the plan from the individual union members through whatever means they choose. The attorney will have no direct contact with the union members unless and until someone decides to use the legal services and contacts the attorney themselves.

D. Referrals

Attorneys are prohibited from paying for referrals except under specific circumstances. Referrals are defined as any recommendation as to the attorney's character, professional ability, or legal competence. This does not include simple directory listings that indicate an attorney's area of practice or expertise, so long as the listing does not include an endorsement for the attorney.

There are, however, some circumstances under which an attorney can pay certain costs with regard to referrals. Attorneys are permitted to pay for reasonable advertising costs, such as fees associated with inclusion in a directory, television and radio airtime, internet advertising and web domain expenses, and print advertising. Employees, vendors, and other representatives—such as public-relations personnel, spokespersons, television and radio actors, and publicists—may be compensated for their services.

The rules also allow for small gifts to be given to a person who recommends the attorney's firm or services. However, the gift must be nothing more than a token, such as a holiday gift or a token of social hospitality.

Attorneys are permitted to use and pay for lead-generating services, such as a qualified, unbiased lawyer referral service, so long as the service does not make specific claims, recommendations, or assertions as to the attorney's abilities, character, or competence. The service may not make any analysis of the person's potential legal issues, may not use a client's information to decide which attorney should receive the lead, and cannot make any claims as to the quality of the services provided by the attorney. It is the attorney's responsibility to ensure that any lead generation or lawyer referral service follows the established rules and professional obligations with regard to referrals.

Reciprocal referral arrangements are permitted so long as such arrangements do not impact the attorney's professional obligations and judgment. Reciprocal arrangements can be between the attorney and any other attorney or non-attorney party. For example, a real estate attorney may have a reciprocal relationship with a local real estate agent. The agent will refer clients to the attorney for their real estate needs, and, in exchange, the attorney will refer clients who require real estate services to the agent. Such an arrangement cannot be exclusive, and neither party can pay for the referrals from the other party. Additionally, clients of both parties must be informed of the reciprocal arrangement and be permitted to seek services elsewhere should they choose. Finally, reciprocal arrangements cannot create any type of conflict of interest and should be reviewed regularly to ensure continued alignment with the appropriate governing rules and policies.

E. Communications Regarding Fields of Practice and Specialization

Attorneys must take care not to misrepresent themselves concerning their particular fields, areas of practice, or specializations. Attorneys may advertise that they specialize in a particular field based on their education and experience, but such claims must not violate the rule barring any false or misleading claims of service.

Attorneys may not claim certification in any particular area of expertise unless the attorney has been formally certified by an approved authority. Formal certification indicates that an authorized, objective agency or organization has verified that the attorney has knowledge, skill, or ability in the area of expertise that is beyond the scope of the general license obtained by all practicing attorneys.

Such certifications must usually be approved by the state where the attorney is licensed and practices law, in the District of Columbia, or in US territory. Certification programs may also be accredited by the American Bar Association, the state supreme court, or the state bar association. Organizations that offer specialized certifications are required to hold applicants to higher degrees of experience, knowledge, and competence than is traditionally expected of general law education and licensure. The certifications rule does not prohibit attorneys from indicating that they practice before the Patent and Trademark Office or that they are Admiralty law firms if they practice maritime law. Both of these designations have

53

a longstanding historical tradition and are not subject to the requirements of formal certification programs.

When claiming such certification in marketing or other communications, the attorney must include the name of the certifying authority in the communication to provide consumers with the means to research the certification and the attorney's credentials. Additionally, any communication is required to contain contact information for the attorney and/or the attorney's law firm. This contact information includes a physical mailing address or office location, a website, email address, and a telephone number.

Domain XI - Lawyers' Duties to the Public and the Legal System

A. Voluntary Pro Bono Service

With regard to legal work, the term "pro bono" means "without charge." Attorneys practicing in the United States are expected to dedicate a certain amount of time to working for the disadvantaged without charging legal fees. While this service is voluntary, it is considered a professional responsibility.

Attorneys are expected to engage in at least fifty hours of pro bono work annually. Depending on the circumstances, some states may expect a greater time commitment, and the number of hours may vary annually. However, over the course of a career, attorneys are expected to meet this average annual commitment. Providing pro bono work is also expected of judges and government attorneys who are not typically permitted to practice law outside of their designated employment. These people can, however, provide pro bono work in the form of education, training, and mentorship. While pro bono work is strongly encouraged, insufficient pro bono work is not meant to be enforced through disciplinary measures.

The majority of pro bono hours should be spent working for the poor and/or charitable, educational, religious, or civic organizations whose primary goal is to support people of limited means. Pro bono work can consist of providing legal representation, providing legal advice, mentoring, participating in training or educational programs, or participating in activities that are intended to improve the law or legal system, such as lobbying or writing administrative rules. Attorneys are also expected to contribute financially to organizations that provide reduced or free legal aid to the indigent whenever feasible.

Pro Bono Responsibility

The phrase "pro bono" means "without charge." Attorneys can provide pro bono services in a number of ways:

Providing free or reduced-fee legal representation.

Providing legal services to charitable organizations that support the indigent.

Dedicating time to mentoring, training, or educational services.

Working to improve the law or legal system.

55

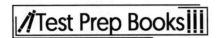

B. Accepting Appointments

Legal representation is part of every citizen's right in the United States, even when they cannot afford to hire a lawyer on their own. In addition, attorneys are usually permitted the free selection of clients and can opt not to represent someone with whom they do not agree or feel as though they cannot effectively represent. However, as part of their pro bono responsibilities, attorneys may sometimes need to represent unpopular or difficult matters or deal with trying or distasteful clients.

As part of the right to representation guaranteed under the justice system, courts must appoint attorneys to represent clients who cannot otherwise provide their own legal representation. Attorneys are expected to accept such appointments even when they would rather not handle the particular matter or represent that particular client.

There are, however, a few circumstances in which an attorney can ask to be excused from an assignment in a given case. For example, if an attorney who routinely handles criminal cases is assigned to represent a client in a complex civil matter, the attorney may feel that they lack the appropriate knowledge and experience to adequately represent the client and may ask to be excused from appointment.

Another instance for asking to refuse an appointment would be in the case of an undue financial burden. High-profile murder trials, for example, usually require a great deal of time, work, and personnel, and it may not be financially feasible for a small, single-attorney practice to handle such an involved and lengthy case.

Finally, attorneys can ask to be excused from representing a client when the client or the case is so repulsive to the attorney that the attorney would not be able to set feelings aside and adequately and effectively represent the client. This last instance may be difficult for a judge to accept, however, and the circumstances surrounding this type of request must be compelling.

C. Serving in Legal Services Organizations

Lawyers are encouraged to participate in legal services organizations, including serving as directors, officers, or board members. Such service does not create attorney-client relationships within the organization or with clients served by the organization. However, the attorney must take care that serving in such a position does not create a conflict of interest with the clients that the attorney represents. In matters involving the organization and in which the attorney's client is directly involved in opposition to the organization or would be materially affected by the organization, the attorney must take extra care not to be involved in decisions for the organization that could negatively affect their client.

D. Law Reform Activities Affecting Client Interests

Attorneys sometimes work with legal reform organizations and/or participate in law reform activities, such as lobbying for a change to a law or the legal system or writing laws or rules that may affect changes to the laws or legal system. These activities can sometimes affect the attorney's client, either positively or negatively, but this does not automatically create an ethics violation. However, the attorney should notify the organization of the attorney-client relationship, without disclosing the identity of the client, when the client could benefit from such reform or legislation. For example, if an

attorney is working on new antitrust legislation while also representing a client who may benefit from the outcome of such legislation, the attorney should disclose this information to the organization working on the legislation. Relationships that may be negatively affected by the attorney's legal reform work need not be disclosed.

E. Criticism of Judges and Adjudicating Officials

The opinions of attorneys and other legal professionals are often taken into consideration when determining the advancement, promotion, or election of certain public legal offices, such as public defenders, prosecutors, and attorneys general. In an effort to maintain professionalism and integrity, attorneys should express their valid, substantiated legal opinions honestly and candidly. Attorneys should refrain from public criticism of judges and adjudicating officials when the information is known to be false or without regard to the validity of such information. Additionally, attorneys should seek to defend courts and judges who are unfairly criticized.

F. Political Contributions to Obtain Engagements or Appointments

As citizens, attorneys have the right to participate in the political system, including making donations, soliciting donations, and committing support to political candidates. This can include providing gifts, loans, or anything of value to a campaign, candidate, or political party. However, attorneys must not undermine the integrity of the legal system by performing such activities when the attorney stands to gain legal work or appointments from such engagements. Similarly, attorneys must not accept political or legal appointments or engagements that are a direct result of political contributions or activities. Appointments based on professional qualifications and expertise, appointments or engagements made on a rotating basis from a predetermined list, and those that are largely uncompensated (such as pro bono assignments) are exempt from this rule. Political donations in exchange for legal engagements are considered to be professional misconduct at the least and may constitute a punishable crime.

G. Improper Influence on Government Officials

Attorneys generally hold a great deal of influence, both with their clients and also within their communities. Part of an attorney's professional conduct responsibilities includes avoiding using that influence to improperly coerce, persuade, or otherwise affect the work and decisions of government officials. Additionally, attorneys may not state nor imply that they have some sort of influence over an official due to any type of relationship or familiarity with that person. For example, an attorney may not tell his client that he can get the charges against the client dropped because the attorney plays golf with the judge's son. That would be claiming improper influence over a government official, whether it is true or not.

H. Assisting Judicial Misconduct

Part of the Rules of Professional Conduct addresses an attorney knowingly engaging in, encouraging, or assisting others with engaging in illegal activities or professional misconduct. This includes assisting a judge or court officer with violating the rules of judicial conduct as well as knowingly and deliberately ignoring violations of the rules. Attorneys must not in any way behave in a manner that goes against the Rules of Professional Conduct, even if they are being asked to do so by a judge or elected official. Additionally, if an attorney becomes aware of judicial misconduct or that a judge has violated the rules

of judicial conduct, particularly in such a way that calls into question the judge's fitness for the position, that attorney is responsible for reporting the incident to the appropriate authorities.

Domain XII - Judicial Conduct

Similar to the Model Rules of Professional Conduct prescribed for attorneys, there is a separate canon of rules specifically addressing the professional conduct expectations for judges. This is known as the Model Code of Judicial Conduct, and its purpose is to promote integrity, professionalism, and public confidence in the judiciary. There are four canons—or general guiding principles—governing judicial conduct, and the overall goal is to protect three key aspects of the judiciary: integrity, impartiality, and independence. These are explicitly stated in Canon 1, which maintains that judges must promote the independence, integrity, and impartiality of the judiciary at all times and must avoid even the appearance of impropriety. Canon 2 states that judges must perform their duties competently and with impartiality. Canon 3 requires judges to actively avoid conflicts of interest between their personal and extracurricular activities and their judiciary responsibilities. Lastly, Canon 4 regulates judicial participation in political campaigns and activities. There are several rules and guidelines within each canon, including the key rules discussed here.

A. Maintaining the Independence and Impartiality of the Judiciary

Canon 1 requires that a judge maintain the "independence, integrity, and impartiality of the judiciary" along with deliberately taking steps to avoid even the appearance of impropriety within the judiciary. It is expected that judges will be under a higher degree of scrutiny than the average citizen and that they represent their position in the legal system even when they are outside of the courtroom. As such, judges are expected to comply at all times with the law as well as with the Code of Judicial Conduct. Judges should seek to promote public confidence in the judicial system in both their professional and personal behavior. In addition to direct violations of the law or orders of the court, improprieties could also include behavior that could cause a reasonable person to question that judge's integrity, impartiality, temperament, or honesty. In addition to maintaining appropriate behavior and ethical standards, judges should also participate in outreach activities and programs that promote the public's understanding of the judicial system, thus helping to maintain public confidence in the system.

Finally, judges should not abuse their position. The position of judge holds a certain amount of authority and prestige within the community, and judges must not use that position to advance their own interests, either personal or financial. For example, a judge should not use their position to coerce a *maître d'* to circumvent the reservation system to give the judge prime seats at a restaurant. Judges must also not use their position to benefit others in this way. Helping a friend avoid paying fines on a traffic ticket, for example, is a violation of judicial conduct and could even constitute a type of bribery should the person ever come into legal issues before the judge's court.

Judges should also avoid using any type of letterhead or correspondence that alludes to their position when communicating about personal matters so as to avoid using undue influence over the recipient of the correspondence. Judges may use their judicial stationery to write a letter of recommendation, for example, but they must make it clear that the letter is based on the judge's personal knowledge of the person. Care must be taken to ensure that the recommendation could not be misconstrued as carrying judicial weight or influence.

Special consideration should be given when a judge contributes articles or other writings for publication, regardless of the content of the writing. The judge must take care that the writing cannot be exploited or used by others to promote their own interests through affiliation with the judge or publication. For

example, a judge should maintain control of advertising that could be affiliated with the writing, such as refusing to allow DUI attorneys to advertise in a publication containing an article about the legalities of roadside field sobriety tests written by the judge. Such advertising could make the judge's article appear to be a conflict of interest in DUI cases involving advertising attorneys, or advertising attorneys could try to create an affiliation with the judge to use in a client's case that a field sobriety test was conducted unfairly.

B. Performing the Duties of Judicial Office Impartially, Competently, and Diligently

Canon 2 states specifically that "a judge shall perform the duties of judicial office impartially, competently, and diligently." Several rules within this Canon further explain and detail exactly what this requires. First and foremost, a judge is required to put their position within the judiciary as a priority, giving it precedence over any person or extrajudicial obligations or activities. The second rule states that judges must perform their duties and uphold the law fairly and with impartiality. This means that judges must remain objective in their decisions, holding all parties to the same requirements and standards. They must interpret the law fairly and without regard to personal preferences, biases, or prejudices. In particular, judges must maintain impartiality with regard to the federally protected classes of race, sex, gender, religion, color, and national origin. They must also remain impartial with regard to the non-federally protected classes of socioeconomic status, marital status, and political affiliation. In addition, judges must also prevent attorneys and others in their courtroom from demonstrating biases or personal prejudices. Demonstrating bias in any way, or allowing others in the courtroom to demonstrate bias, risks impacting the fairness of the entire proceedings and calls into question the judge's ability to discharge their duties with impartiality.

Judges must also be competent and diligent in performing their judicial duties. They are expected to maintain current legal knowledge and skill and to be adequately prepared for each case being tried before them. They must manage their time and staff to effectively and efficiently discharge all of the duties of the court. Time must be appropriately allocated for the disposition of the court's business, and judges are expected to be on time and adequately prepared for all matters before the court. Judges must also work with the attorneys to ensure that adequate time is given to all parties to prepare and present their cases thoroughly and effectively while also preventing unnecessary delays and/or costs.

Finally, judges must be able to manage the business of the court with order and dignity. The judge must be patient, professional, and courteous to all parties in the courtroom, including attorneys, litigants, witnesses, jurors, court staff, and officials. Further, the judge must impose a similar code of conduct on attorneys and other participants in the litigation to maintain a fair and impartial courtroom.

C. Ex Parte Communications

The term ex parte means favoring one side over another or giving greater respect or attention to one side as opposed to the other. Ex parte communications refer to discussing matters of the current case with only one side or party to the case without the presence of representatives for the other side. Judges must avoid having any communication with one side of a pending matter (either the plaintiff or the defendant) outside of the presence of the other side. This rule extends to members of the judge's staff, as well. The judge must include all parties or their attorneys when discussing any matters affecting the case.

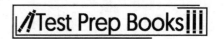

There are some specific circumstances in which the ex parte communications rule is not applicable, but they are few. For example, ex parte communication is permitted in simple matters of scheduling or administrative issues where the communication does not address substantive matters of the case and will not favor either side of the case. The judge must also promptly notify the other party of the communication and allow that party to respond as necessary.

Judges may also seek information or guidance from disinterested third parties so long as the communication does not include a discussion of facts of the case, and both sides are informed of the communication and given the opportunity to respond and object should they wish. Additionally, the outside party must not have any material interest in the case, whether formerly, presently, or prospectively. For example, a judge may seek information or advice from another judge on a matter, but that judge may not have formerly recused themselves from the case nor be an appellate judge who may potentially hear the matter in the future.

Similarly, judges may communicate with their staff as needed, so long as such communication does not materially affect the proceedings. Lastly, with the permission of both parties, ex parte communications are also permitted if the judge is overseeing efforts to mediate or settle the pending litigation.

There is an allowance for instances of inadvertent ex parte communication. For example, if a judge inadvertently comes across information that is substantial to the pending litigation, such as receiving a fax or email communication by mistake, the judge must immediately notify both parties of the substance of the communication and give both parties the opportunity to respond.

There are a few circumstances where ex parte communication is permitted by law. For example, a judge may consult an ethics advisory committee or other legal experts about the judge's compliance with the Judicial Code of Conduct. In this case, the parties to the pending litigation do not need to be consulted nor informed of the communication. Additionally, certain therapeutic courts, such as mental health, drug, or domestic violence courts, actually encourage ex parte communications when the judge is actively engaged in working out solutions to the case, such as discussing treatment options or working with treatment providers or social workers.

D. Disqualification

Judges are disqualified and expected to recuse themselves from any matters in which they may not be able to remain impartial or if their participation could suggest impartiality. There could be many examples of these types of situations, but the Model Code of Judicial Conduct lists six in particular.

First, the judge must recuse or disqualify themselves if they have a personal bias or prejudicial opinion of any party to the case or if the judge has knowledge of facts of the case that are in dispute. For example, a judge cannot hear a case involving their personal attorney if that relationship is current and ongoing. The judge must refrain from hearing cases involving the attorney for at least two years after the dissolution of the attorney-client relationship.

A judge should also recuse themselves from a case involving parties with whom the judge has a familiar relationship (be it a friend, family member, business associate, or other personal relationship). This includes attorneys, litigants, or material witnesses. The familiar relationship extends not only to the judge but also to parties acquainted with the judge's spouse or domestic partner. This also includes

third-degree relationships such as parents, children, and siblings of the judge or the judge's spouse or partner.

Judges are also disqualified from hearing cases in which the judge has prior participation. This includes serving as an attorney or in association with an attorney who was substantially involved in the case or serving as a material witness in the case. Additionally, judges are disqualified if they served as a judge on the case in another court. For example, a new appellate judge is disqualified from hearing a case that the judge presided over in a lower court.

A fourth situation requiring disqualification is one in which the judge has a financial interest, either personally or as a fiduciary. This economic interest can include ownership or financial interest in any party to the proceedings. Disqualification of the judge is required if the financial interest involves the judge's spouse or partner, parent, child, or other family member.

Along similar lines, the judge is disqualified from participating in a case involving parties who have contributed financially to the judge's election campaign. Each state has its own rules specifying the time frame and amount of the contribution that would require recusal. Finally, judges are disqualified if they have made prior public statements about the case where such comments appear to presume how a judge might rule in a proceeding.

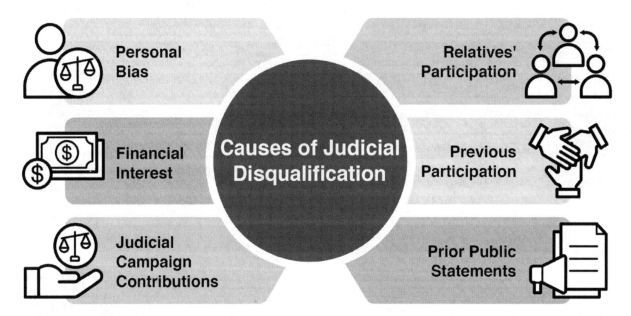

Judicial disqualification can be waived by agreement of both parties, outside the presence of the judge. The judge must disclose the reason for the recusal on the record, and so long as the reason does not involve personal bias and the attorneys agree to waive the disqualification, the judge may participate in the proceedings.

Finally, the rule of necessity allows for the participation of a judge who would otherwise be disqualified based on exceptional circumstances that require the judge's participation in the case. The rule of necessity may come into play in certain emergency situations when no other judge is available to preside. These situations may include emergency temporary restraining order applications in domestic violence situations, for example, or a hearing on probable cause. In these instances, the judge must

include on the record the reason(s) for the disqualification and must transfer the case to another available judge as soon as is reasonably possible.

E. Extrajudicial Activities

Canon 3 addresses the rules concerning a judge's personal and extrajudicial activities. Judges are permitted to teach, write, lecture, and have speaking engagements as part of these activities, and they are permitted to receive payment or compensation for these activities so long as the compensation is reasonable and customary for the task performed. Such income must be reported to the court clerk and posted to the court's website as public notification of income received. The posting must include the type and amount of the compensation; the date, place, and nature of the activity performed; and the source of the compensation.

Judges are allowed to participate in legal or judicial activities, such as participating in conferences, working with the bar association, or teaching at a law school. Judges are also permitted to engage in educational, civic, religious, and charitable activities and may serve as officers, board members, trustees, or non-legal advisors for such organizations, so long as such service is not for profit. Involvement in these types of organizations is limited to those that do not regularly have dealings with the judge's court or jurisdiction. The judge is also not permitted to engage in fundraising nor the solicitation of new members for such organizations.

Judges are also limited in their appearances at public hearings. They may only voluntarily attend hearings when they are providing expertise or knowledge of the law with governmental bodies or officials. They must take care not to use the prestige of their position to influence others or to advance their own interests. They may, however, appear before governing bodies and/or officials on matters that concern the judges as private citizens, such as hearings involving zoning laws or local ordinances.

Regardless of type, personal and extrajudicial activities must not interfere with the judge's responsibilities to the court or their judicial duties. The activities must not negatively impact nor appear to impact the independence, integrity, or impartiality of the court. Additionally, such activities must not appear to be coercive or result in the frequent disqualification of the judge. Finally, the judge may not use the court location, materials, staff, or resources while engaging in personal and extrajudicial activities. All of the exceptions and limitations concerning extrajudicial activities involve maintaining high standards of appropriate judicial conduct.

Practice Test #1

Domain I: Regulation of the Legal Profession

1. An attorney is unsure if information they are given in private by a client could lead to illegal activity. What authority should the attorney consult to determine the correct rules for ethical conduct in this situation?
   a. The American Bar Association's Revised Model Rules of Professional Conduct
   b. The jurisdictional authority
   c. The federal government
   d. Their fellow associates at the law firm

2. At a large law firm that employs a number of lawyers, one attorney asks a colleague to help gather some information about an old case the firm worked on, and the attorney complies without asking what the information would be used for. A few weeks later, the lawyer who was given the information was caught selling the same evidence gathered about the case to another attorney in a different firm. Which lawyer would MOST likely be subjected to disciplinary action for breaking the jurisdiction's code of ethics regarding unscrupulous activity?
   a. All lawyers involved
   b. The lawyer who sold the information and the lawyer who purchased the information
   c. The lawyer who sold the information and the lawyer who helped gather the information
   d. Only the lawyer who sold the information

3. An attorney at a firm finds out that one of their colleagues, who is also an attorney, has been charging a client of theirs two times what other attorneys at the same firm charge for the same service. They are also charging the client for services they did not perform. Which, if any, of these actions is the attorney required to report as misconduct after witnessing?
   a. Charging a client two times the normal service fee
   b. Charging a client for services they did not perform`
   c. Both A and B
   d. None of these actions

4. A client attempts to call his lawyer for consultation on an urgent matter about what information to reveal during an interview. When they call, only the paralegal is available because the lawyer had a personal emergency. The client stresses they need information on how to act now, so they request that the paralegal advise them. What information is the paralegal permitted to give the client?
   a. The paralegal can provide consulting to the best of their abilities for the client.
   b. The paralegal can give the client information that was recently found regarding the case to help influence the client's decision.
   c. The paralegal can ask another lawyer in the firm to provide counsel.
   d. The paralegal must wait until the lawyer can provide legal advice.

5. A longtime client of a lawyer who practices in New York is involved in a personal injury incident while on vacation in another state. How could the lawyer still participate in the case and represent the client if the jurisdiction where the incident took place is in an area the lawyer is not certified in, without having to go through the process of being licensed in another state?

    a. The lawyer would still be qualified to represent the client in a different state.

    b. The lawyer would not be able to assist the client outside their jurisdiction.

    c. The lawyer would need to work with a lawyer who is certified in the jurisdiction, with both lawyers participating actively in the case.

    d. The lawyer would need to marry or be related to another lawyer certified in the state in which they wish to represent the client.

6. An attorney receives a flat rate of $5000 for legal work performed for a client. It is the holiday season, so the lawyer wants to distribute some of this money to his assistants and paralegal team, in addition to their regular compensation. Is the lawyer permitted to divide these funds to his employees in this situation?

    a. Yes. They work under the lawyer, so he can pay them anything he wishes.

    b. Yes. They are involved in the case, so they are entitled to a share of the legal fees.

    c. No. Fee division is not allowed between lawyers and non-lawyers in addition to regular compensation.

    d. No. The lawyer needs to inform the local jurisdiction of his intentions before he can distribute the fees.

7. A manager of a firm instructs a paralegal to give them confidential information that the lawyer they are working for has documented for a case or they will lose their job. What would be the BEST action for the paralegal to take to avoid an ethical violation?

    a. Give the manager the information because the paralegal is required to perform the requests of their manager.

    b. Report the manager to the jurisdictional authority.

    c. Wait to inform the lawyer about the situation for the best course of action.

    d. Only give the manager information the paralegal decides to be unimportant to the case.

Domain II: The Client-Lawyer Relationship

8. An individual calls a law firm and informs them of a case they need assistance with. The firm sets up a consultation with one of their lawyers, and at the meeting more information about the case is revealed. The individual likes the lawyer and decides to hire them for representation, so they draft a written contract, and both parties sign. The client then tells the lawyer all the information about their situation, including possibly incriminating evidence. At what point in the relationship did the information the client was telling the firm and the attorney become confidential?

    a. When the individual called the law firm

    b. When they met for consultation

    c. When they agreed to create a contract with the lawyer

    d. When the client and lawyer signed the contract

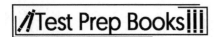

9. A lawyer agrees to represent a client who is suing another individual for copyright infringement and defamation. During the case, while researching information, the attorney realizes they do not have the adequate knowledge of copyright law to be successful in the case, so they inform the client that they want to limit their representation to handling only the defamation aspect of the case. Is the lawyer justified in limiting the scope of their representation in this case?

    a. Yes. The lawyer can limit their scope at any time if they find they cannot fully complete their client's requests.

    b. Yes. The lawyer can work as much or as little of the case as they like as long as they do not charge fees for incomplete work.

    c. No. Only the jurisdiction can limit the scope of a lawyer's capabilities.

    d. No. The lawyer needs to give up representation and compensate the client accordingly for breaking their contract.

10. A client in a criminal case has already decided to plead not guilty and understands the consequences of his decision. However, the client is unsure if taking the case to a trial by jury will help their situation. Therefore, they attempt to defer the decision to their attorney, who has years of experience representing clients in similar situations. Is the lawyer permitted to make this decision for their client?

    a. Yes. The client has already established a plea and therefore can defer the remaining decisions to their attorney.

    b. Yes. The client has a right to defer the decision to have a trial by jury to their attorney in any situation.

    c. No. The judge determines when a jury trial takes place.

    d. No. The trial by jury is a decision of actual authority that the client must make.

11. A prospective client confesses to a lawyer that they are thinking of illegally taking advantage of a bank by wiring money to themselves through an unnoticed system. The individual then asks the lawyer if they can consult on the different punishments that might result from their actions. Is the lawyer permitted to give the individual this information?

    a. Yes, as long as the lawyer does not assist in committing the crime.

    b. Yes, as long as the lawyer and client share the profits.

    c. No. The lawyer cannot assist in giving any information to potential criminals.

    d. No. The lawyer and prospective client must sign a contract before agreeing to exchange information.

12. A few nights before their trial is set to start, the client, scared of the outcome, becomes angry and ends up pushing the attorney down. The fall does not result in serious injury, but the attorney is upset with the client and fears another outburst, leading to a desire to end his work for the client without completing the case. Would the attorney be permitted to terminate the lawyer-client relationship?

    a. Yes. The client was physically violent toward the attorney.

    b. Yes. The lawyer does not need a reason to end the lawyer-client relationship.

    c. No. It is too close to the trial date and leaving the client would cause considerable hardship for them.

    d. No. The act was not serious enough to warrant dismissing the case.

13. An individual speaks to an attorney over the phone as a prospective client, giving information about a trademark they need to have filed. The individual verbally agrees to a $50 hourly rate for the service, and the lawyer begins the work. However, when the lawyer bills the client, the client claims they did not realize they were fully agreeing to the amount because it was not in writing, and they refuse to submit payment to the lawyer. Is the client still required to pay the fees in this case?
    a. Yes. If a lawyer performs work for a case, they are permitted to ask for payment at any time.
    b. Yes. A contract was verbally formed and needs to be adhered to.
    c. No. The contract was not official until it was written and signed.
    d. No. The lawyer-client relationship had not been formed when they were discussing fees.

14. A lawyer realizes a case they accepted is requiring a lot more work than they expected; therefore, the attorney wants to hire more team members to help with research and paperwork for the case. Would the lawyer be required to contact the client before making this decision?
    a. Yes. The client needs to be informed before the lawyer makes any decision on their case.
    b. Yes. The relationship was already established with a set number of employees.
    c. No. The lawyer is entitled to make their own decisions regarding staffing for a case at any time.
    d. No. The lawyer can make any decisions that they are not specified to defer to the client in the lawyer-client contract.

15. A lawyer decides to take up a client in a criminal case who does not have the immediate funds to pay the legal fees because the client agrees to a high contingency percentage. However, legal expenses still arise over the course of working on the case. Which of the following would the lawyer be permitted to do to cover expenses of the legal case until contingency can be obtained?
    a. Accept a lien from the client.
    b. Loan the client the money for legal expenses.
    c. Require a third party to pay all legal fees and the client to pay the contingency.
    d. A contingency fee would not be allowed in this situation.

Domain III: Client Confidentiality

16. An individual meets someone through a mutual friend at a party who works as an attorney. The individual speaks with the attorney about a problem they have been thinking of hiring a lawyer for, describing their situation and consulting the lawyer about what type of services the attorney would be willing to offer and what the fees might be. After the conversation, the individual expresses that some of the details he spoke about the case should not be repeated. Would the information exchanged be protected under the attorney-client privilege?
    a. Yes. When the individual began to consult with the lawyer, the information became confidential.
    b. Yes. When the attorney described their fees, they were creating a contract.
    c. No. The information was not agreed to be confidential beforehand.
    d. No. The attorney was not practicing law when the information was exchanged.

17. An individual who was interviewed regarding evidence for a dispute dies during an ongoing case. However, before the individual's death, a lawyer gathered and documented important evidence from the interview. Some of the information was considered to be incriminating to their client, so they decide to not disclose the information. However, the prosecuting attorney says the information still needs to be disclosed because it contains evidence that cannot be obtained from anywhere but the lawyer's work-product doctrine. Is the work-product doctrine allowed to be used as evidence in this dispute?

    a. Yes. There is no other way to obtain the information other than through the work-product document.

    b. Yes. A lawyer can share or borrow any documents they wish from other attorneys.

    c. No. The information is protected and confidential as work-product doctrine.

    d. No. The prosecution needs to get permission from a relative of the deceased person before the information can be disclosed.

18. Which of the following information would NOT be considered confidential in a lawyer-client relationship?

    a. Information discussed in a meeting between a client, their lawyer, and a friend of the client

    b. Pretrial notes written by an attorney

    c. Research by a paralegal for a case

    d. Information about a case discussed during a consultation between a lawyer and a potential client

19. During a criminal trial for burglary, a client wishes to disclose confidential information about how he was forced into committing the crime, but the attorney advises him against disclosing the information because it could hurt his chances of being acquitted. However, the client is insistent and requests that the confidential information be told to the court by the lawyer. Is the lawyer obligated to disclose the information?

    a. Yes. The lawyer must obey the requests of their client.

    b. Yes. The information is not confidential.

    c. No. The lawyer can decide against a decision that might cause them to lose the case.

    d. No. The lawyer is in charge of decision making during a trial.

20. A client opens a dispute after losing a domestic case about the amount of work their lawyer did to support their objectives. The client claims the lawyer did not perform enough preparatory work for the client's defense. The lawyer claims they have a work-product doctrine that proves they were documenting evidence and preparing diligent notes for the duration of the case. However, the documents contain information that is confidential to the client. Is the lawyer allowed to use their work-product doctrine as evidence in the case?

    a. Yes. When the case ends, all related documents can be released.

    b. Yes. The documents are in defense of claims brought against the lawyer.

    c. No. The work-product doctrine is confidential and not allowed to be used at any time against the client.

    d. No. The contract formed before beginning the case did not state that the information could be disclosed.

Domain IV: Conflicts of Interest

21. After agreeing to represent two different clients in unrelated cases at the same time, an attorney realizes they do not have enough time to complete all the work involved. Which of the following would the lawyer be permitted to do to ensure there is not a multiple-client conflict?
    a. Complete the shorter case as quickly as they can so they can focus on the longer case.
    b. Dedicate their time to the neediest client.
    c. Hire paralegal staff and assistants to work on one of the cases while focusing on the other.
    d. Terminate one of the relationships and compensate them for any damages.

22. A lawyer represents a car manufacturer in a dispute involving the company and one of its employees. Since it's near the holidays, the car manufacturer offers the lawyer a stationary set as a token of their thanks. Is the lawyer permitted to accept the gift according to the profession's ethical guidelines?
    a. Yes. The gift is related to the case.
    b. Yes. The gift was not solicited by the attorney.
    c. No. The gift is of too much significant value.
    d. No. The lawyer cannot accept any type of gift that is not first agreed to in the lawyer-client contract.

23. After consulting with a prospective client, an attorney discovers that the individual is related to a client they represented several years earlier. When researching the documents of the past case, the lawyer discovers some information he could possibly use to benefit the prospective client. Is the lawyer permitted to represent the prospective client and disclose their relative's case information?
    a. Yes. The clients are related, so they can be given information about each other's cases.
    b. Yes. When the case was finished, the information lost its obligation to remain confidential.
    c. No. The attorney cannot represent parties related to former clients.
    d. No. The former client's information is still confidential.

24. An attorney meets with a prospective client at their office who gives them specific information about a case, and both parties agree to formally draft a written contract. However, the prospective client later decides they want to use a different attorney and ends up not signing any agreements. The opposing party to the client in the dispute then calls the attorney, requesting consultation and possible representation. Can the lawyer represent this new client?
    a. Yes, as long as the lawyer does not reveal information discussed between them and the former prospective client.
    b. Yes. The contract was not finalized, so the lawyer is still free to represent any party they wish.
    c. No. If the attorney hears any details that could be used against a prospective client, they are no longer allowed to represent any party other than that party.
    d. No. The contract was already being drafted, so the lawyer and client have to follow the contract.

25. A lawyer who works at a large firm is approached by a prospective client who is disputing a decision made in a case that another lawyer at the firm prosecuted the client for in the past. However, the lawyer of the current prospective client does not come into contact with the lawyer who worked the past case, and they have never met due to the size of the firm. Therefore, the attorney still wants to represent the client and decides to try and have the other attorney screened from the case. Is the lawyer entitled to represent the prospective client if they screen the past attorney from participation?

    a. Yes, as long as the two lawyers do not discuss any information about either case to one another.
    b. Yes. The lawyer does not speak to or know the other attorney who worked the past case.
    c. No. There would still be an imputed conflict due to the relationship between the two cases.
    d. No. Both lawyers have to participate in the current case.

26. An attorney finds out that a business they have invested in is involved in a dispute. The lawyer wants to represent the business in the case to try and make sure the company does not lose money, so they approach the business and offer a relatively low flat fee for representation. Is the lawyer permitted to represent the business in this case?

    a. Yes. The lawyer is free to choose who they wish to represent as long as the terms are agreed upon.
    b. Yes. The dispute gives extra motivation for the attorney to work harder to win their client's case.
    c. No. A lawyer is not permitted to work a case in which the litigation could benefit the attorney.
    d. No. The lawyer cannot solicit their representation to a business.

27. Which of the following would be considered an unethical business transaction between a lawyer and their client?

    a. A verbal agreement to pay a given hourly fee
    b. A verbal agreement to pay contingency fees
    c. A billing for fees agreed to in a contract
    d. The lawyer requiring the client to pay a retainer fee before representation

28. An attorney decides to represent a client that is a founding member of a very large and prosperous corporation, and an agreement is made for the client to pay a flat rate for representation. When the bill is requested to be paid by the client, the client informs the attorney that their business handles all their expenses. However, when contacted, the business says they had no knowledge of the case or bill. Is the lawyer permitted to still request and collect the payment from the company the individual is a part of in this situation?

    a. Yes. Because the client is a founding member, they can request that their business take care of their payments.
    b. Yes. The lawyer can take payment for the case from whoever is willing to give it.
    c. No. The attorney did not send a copy of the contract or billing information to the business first.
    d. No. The third party needs to be mentioned in the contract.

29. Which of the following situations would prevent an attorney from representing a private client in a criminal case?

    a. The attorney worked as a government lawyer for a previous case the client was involved in.
    b. The attorney is married to the client.
    c. The attorney just finished law school.
    d. The attorney is already involved in another, unrelated private case.

Domain V: Competence, Legal Malpractice, and Other Civil Liability

30. Which of the following is NOT an example of how an attorney can maintain competence?
    a. Taking educational courses on changing law practices
    b. Purchasing new software for faster data collection
    c. Attending a training seminar offered by the attorney's firm
    d. Outsourcing work to specialized firms

31. A new attorney is approached by an individual for representation during a divorce proceeding. However, the attorney has only ever worked on a divorce case as a paralegal during schooling, and they have not represented a client in a divorce as a lead attorney. Is the attorney permitted to represent the client in this case?
    a. Yes, as long as the attorney discloses their lack of experience.
    b. Yes, if the attorney asks the local jurisdiction first.
    c. No. The attorney does not have enough experience to adequately represent the client.
    d. No. The attorney would need to be licensed specifically as a divorce lawyer.

32. A client expresses a desire to release information to the court that the attorney believes might hurt their case. However, the attorney concedes with the client's request without questioning or informing the client of the possible danger. The case is eventually lost, and the client attempts to accuse the attorney of malpractice for not making enough effort to win. Would the lawyer be guilty of malpractice?
    a. Yes. The attorney should have advised the client not to release the possibly damaging information.
    b. Yes. The attorney did not gather enough evidence.
    c. No. The attorney was doing their job by performing their client's requests.
    d. No. The circumstances that lost them the case were outside the attorney's powers.

33. An attorney is found guilty of malpractice while representing a company. One of the organization's board members who was not directly represented is also demanding reparations for the monetary losses they incurred as a result. Is the attorney subject to civil liability from the nonclient?
    a. Yes. The board member was considered an indirect client of the lawyer, so they are entitled to a portion of the settlement.
    b. Yes. If an attorney's actions result in damages to a related party, the attorney can be subject to civil liability from the nonclient.
    c. No. An attorney cannot be subjected to civil liability from a nonclient.
    d. No. The party was not mentioned in the lawyer-client contract.

34. A client approaches an attorney with a desperate case they have little chance of winning. When negotiating a lawyer-client contract, the attorney says they will agree to represent the client as long as they are permitted to do whatever they like without the chance of being accused of malpractice, and the client agrees. Would their contract be considered valid?
    a. Yes. The client and attorney both agreed to the terms.
    b. Yes. The case involved a considerable amount of risk, so the attorney was permitted to limit their liability for malpractice.
    c. No. The attorney would not be allowed to limit their liability for malpractice in this instance.
    d. No. An attorney is not permitted to accept cases that do not have a considerable chance of success.

71

35. Which of the following methods would a lawyer NOT be permitted to use to mitigate the damage of a malpractice claim?
   a. Disclosing work product doctrine
   b. Using malpractice insurance
   c. A contract that sets the amount of reparations a client can receive from a malpractice claim
   d. Hiring specialized malpractice attorneys

Domain VI: Litigation and Other Forms of Advocacy

36. A client presents a criminal case they have very little information about to an attorney. Is the attorney allowed to accept the case without knowing all the circumstances involved?
   a. Yes. The attorney can gather more information on the case as it progresses.
   b. Yes. The attorney can represent anyone in any situation they are approached with if it will make them and their firm profit.
   c. No. There is not enough information about the case to ensure the attorney has the right skills and experience to provide adequate representation.
   d. No. The chance the case will be lost is too great.

37. A client expresses that they want their case to be finished within a few days. However, when the time is up, the attorney feels they do not have enough evidence to support the case and asks the client to postpone the litigation until more information can be gained. The client does not agree and wants the litigation expedited. Is the attorney permitted to postpone litigation in this instance?
   a. Yes, because it will help the client's case.
   b. Yes, as long as the completion dates were not stated in the contract.
   c. No. Postponement would create an unfair advantage against the opposition.
   d. No. The attorney must obey the client's requests.

38. During a trial, a lawyer makes a statement that they later discover is false. However, the information helps their client's case, and the client tells the lawyer to not disclose the true information. Is the lawyer still required to correct the statement?
   a. Yes. A lawyer must always retract any false information given to a tribunal.
   b. Yes. Decisions to change or retract information made to a tribunal are up to the lawyer, not the client.
   c. No. The attorney believed the information was true when they gave it.
   d. No. The attorney must do as their client requests.

39. An attorney is presented with evidence obtained by one of their paralegal assistants that could be harmful to their client's case. The attorney instructs their assistant to hide the evidence and pretend they never presented it to the attorney. However, the case is still lost. Could the attorney be subjected to malpractice?
   a. Yes. An attorney is not allowed to instruct their team to hide or destroy any evidence in a case.
   b. Yes. All incriminating evidence must be disclosed to the tribunal, regardless of how it was found.
   c. No. The assistant ultimately hid the evidence, not the attorney.
   d. No. The information was not important enough because the case was still lost.

40. After a case has been decided, an attorney who represented the losing party tries to speak with a juror for information about their decision in order to gain evidence to use for a future appeal. However, immediately following the trial, the juror, in a hurry, briefly expresses they do not want to talk. Is the attorney still permitted to pursue discussion at a later date if it will help their client's chances for an appeal?
    a. Yes. There was no contractual agreement that stated they could not peruse a discussion about the case.
    b. Yes. The attorney is permitted to attempt as many discussions as they wish in order to obtain evidence in support of their client.
    c. No. The attorney is never permitted to speak to jurors after a case has ended.
    d. No. Once a juror signifies that they do not want to speak with the attorney, the attorney is no longer permitted to pursue any further discussion.

41. An attorney is permitted to use which of the following methods to convince a tribunal to make a decision in favor of their client?
    a. Forming a contractual agreement with the proceeding judge
    b. Speaking privately with a juror
    c. Using persuasive evidence in favor of their client
    d. Twisting facts of a situation to better fit the position of the attorney's client

42. An attorney agrees to represent a client who is accused of murder and considered potentially dangerous by the state. The client expresses to the attorney that they do not want their situation or identity exposed to the public or in any type of media outlet. However, while awaiting trial, the client disappears. Would the lawyer then be required to disclose information about their client to the public?
    a. Yes. The public is entitled to any information about criminal court cases.
    b. Yes. Because the individual could be dangerous, the attorney must disclose any information that could keep the public out of harm.
    c. No. The attorney must still do what was instructed of them by the client and refrain from disclosing any of the client's information to the public.
    d. No. The information is still considered confidential and should never be disclosed without the client's consent.

43. In which of the following situations would a lawyer NOT be permitted to act as a witness?
    a. During a trial in which they are representing one of the parties involved to detail the type and scope of their work completed for the client
    b. During a trial in which they are representing one of the parties involved to help their client's case
    c. During a trial they are not a part of but in which an attorney from their firm is representing a client
    d. When giving evidence for a client who is financially unable to find new representation

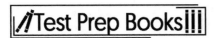

Domain VII: Transactions and Communications with Persons Other Than Clients
44. A lawyer discovers evidence that might hurt their client's case. Is the lawyer allowed to withhold this information from the court?
  a. Yes, as long as the attorney does not try to hide or destroy the evidence.
  b. Yes, if the jurisdiction first approves the withholding of the information.
  c. No. All relevant facts must be disclosed to all parties involved in the case upon discovery.
  d. No. Only the client can determine what information is withheld.

45. The opposing party of an attorney's client wishes to discuss the case in a meeting with the attorney. The attorney's client agrees to allow the meeting, as both feel it could expedite a settlement in favor of the client. Is the attorney allowed to meet with the opposing party?
  a. Yes. Their client permitted the discussion.
  b. Yes. The lawyer can discuss the case with any party if it might help their client's position.
  c. No. The attorney is never permitted to exchange information related to a case with a party who is already represented by another attorney in a dispute.
  d. No. The attorney did not first obtain the permission of the opposing party's lawyer.

46. During a high-profile case in which most of the details are known by the media, which of the following parties is a lawyer permitted to discuss the case with?
  a. The opposing party
  b. An unrepresented person involved in the dispute
  c. The local media
  d. The opposing party's attorney

Domain VIII: Different Roles of the Lawyer
47. Which of the following is NOT one of the roles of a lawyer?
  a. Advisor
  b. Juror
  c. Negotiator
  d. Arbitrator

48. A lawyer is requested to act as a mediator between two opposing parties in a dispute. However, one of the parties is not represented by an attorney. The unrepresented party asks for advice from the lawyer acting as the mediator. Is the lawyer permitted to provide counsel to the unrepresented party?
  a. Yes, as long as the opposing attorney allows it.
  b. Yes, as long as the counsel does not give unfair advantage to the opposing party.
  c. No. A lawyer acting as a mediator is prohibited from giving advice or counsel to any party during a settlement.
  d. No. The lawyer would have to be acting as an arbitrator, not a mediator.

49. A lawyer is chosen to represent a publicly owned corporation in a dispute against another business. One of the board members chosen to represent the corporation and communicate with the lawyer requests that the attorney disclose confidential information that could be used against the corporation to the media for the individual's personal benefit. Is the attorney required to disclose the information?
   a. Yes. The attorney must do what any of the members of the corporation they are representing request.
   b. Yes. The media is entitled to information related to a case involving a publicly owned corporation.
   c. No. Confidential information should never be disclosed to anyone who is not part of the corporation being represented.
   d. No. An attorney is allowed to make their own decisions in support of the entire corporation if one of the members is requesting action that could hurt the group's case.

Domain IX: Safekeeping Funds and Other Property

50. Attorney A received a security retainer from a client over the weekend. He was going to be in court all of the following week, so he left the money with a note to his secretary to deposit the funds into the practice's main account for safekeeping until the attorney could get to the bank to set up a trust account the following week. Did Attorney A act in a fiduciary manner concerning the client's funds?
   a. Yes, the money will be safe in the bank until the attorney can set up an appropriate account.
   b. Yes, the secretary is responsible for managing the practice and could be trusted to safeguard the funds.
   c. No, the funds cannot be commingled with the attorney's funds, even temporarily.
   d. No, the secretary cannot be responsible for the money.

51. Client Smith has paid a $5,000 security retainer to Attorney Jones, who puts the funds into a trust account. At the resolution of the case, Client Smith disputes the number of hours that Attorney Jones has billed and demands the return of those funds. What is the appropriate course of action for Attorney Jones?
   a. Attorney Jones must place the disputed funds into a joint trust account pending the resolution of the dispute.
   b. Attorney Jones must return the funds to the client and then submit a bill to the client for the remaining money owed.
   c. Attorney Jones may keep the earned monies but must provide a detailed statement to Client Smith.
   d. Client Smith has no recourse as the security retainer was paid to cover Attorney Jones' fees.

52. What steps must an attorney take when assuming possession of a client's property?
   a. The attorney must have the property appraised for value, then kept in a secure location, and must notify all interested parties that the property is in the attorney's possession.
   b. The attorney must notify all parties within fourteen days of receipt of the property.
   c. The property must be disbursed promptly upon resolution of the case.
   d. The property must be identified and labeled, the item must be put into a secure location, and all parties must be notified that the item is in the attorney's possession.

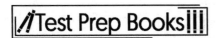

Domain X: Communications about Legal Services

53. Which Supreme Court case maintained the rights of attorneys to advertise their services as an extension of the attorneys' First Amendment rights?
    a. Virginia Board of Pharmacists v. Virginia Citizens' Consumer Council
    b. Alexander v. Cahill
    c. Bates v. State Bar of Arizona
    d. Zauderer v. Office of Disciplinary Counsel

54. Attorney A is writing an advertisement introducing his new law firm to publish in the local newspaper. He plans to include the names, addresses, and telephone numbers of all of his attorneys, as well as their state bar admission dates. He also has several regular clients who will be clients of his new firm, and he plans to include their names, as well. In addition, he will be publishing his firm's initial consultation fees and the range of fees for several of the services the firm will offer. Finally, two of his attorneys were born in the area, so Attorney A will highlight that they are "locals." Which part of Attorney A's advertisement could be a violation of the advertising rules?
    a. The attorneys' bar admission dates
    b. The names of regular clients
    c. The birthplace of the attorneys
    d. The law firm's fees

55. Attorney Q has become aware of a person who was involved in a serious car accident and has been hospitalized. Attorney Q would like to offer his legal services to this person because he has prior experience handling this type of case as well as experience working with the involved insurance companies. What is the best way for Attorney Q to contact the potential client?
    a. Mailing a letter to the potential client
    b. Calling the person on the phone
    c. Visiting the potential client in the hospital
    d. Visiting the person at his home

56. Attorney K, a senior partner in ABC Law Firm, has come to an agreement with the CEO of XYZ Company to offer a legal services subscription package to the employees of XYZ. Now that an agreement has been reached, who can contact the employees to offer enrollment in the program?
    a. Attorney K
    b. Attorneys employed by ABC Law Firm
    c. No direct contact is permitted; employees must decide to enroll on their own.
    d. The HR department of XYZ

Domain XI: Lawyer's Duties to the Public and the Legal System Questions

57. Attorney Q has been assigned a pro bono case in which the defendant is being accused of a violent double homicide. Attorney Q does have some experience in criminal law and has not completed her pro bono hours for the year. However, her law firm is very small, and murder cases take a great deal of time and resources to try. Can Attorney Q ask to be excused from assignment to this particular case?
    a. No, she has not yet completed her required pro bono hours and must accept the assignment.
    b. No, she has the necessary experience to handle this type of case.
    c. Yes, a case of this magnitude would put undue financial strain on her law firm.
    d. Yes, attorneys can request to be excused from any case for any reason so long as they serve their pro bono requirements in some way.

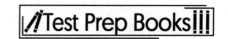

Domain XII: Judicial Conduct Questions

58. What are the four canons of rules that are specifically applicable to judges called?
    a. Model Rules of Professional Conduct
    b. Model Code of Professional Conduct
    c. Model Rules of Judicial Conduct
    d. Model Code of Judicial Conduct

59. Tony, a law clerk, has asked Judge Jones to write him a letter of recommendation for his application to law school. Judge Jones agrees to write the letter and uses both his judicial letterhead as well as his title in the correspondence. Is this appropriate?
    a. Yes, judicial letterhead and titles are not regulated within the code of behavior.
    b. Yes, judicial letterhead and titles may be used in letters of recommendation so long as the judge has personal knowledge of the person.
    c. No, using the letterhead would constitute a misuse of the judge's position and influence.
    d. No, judges are not permitted to write letters of recommendation except in a personal situation without reference to their position.

60. Judge Williams was inadvertently copied on an ex parte email from the prosecutorial team in a case that is pending before his court. What should he do?
    a. He should disregard and delete the email immediately.
    b. He should forward the email to the defense team so that all parties have the same information.
    c. He must immediately notify both parties and give both parties the opportunity to respond.
    d. He must recuse himself from the case as the communication could be considered undue influence from the prosecution.

Answer Explanations #1

Domain I: Regulation of the Legal Profession

1. B: The jurisdiction a lawyer is licensed to work under would be the ultimate rulemaking authority on matters of ethics for the practice of law in the area. Even if these rules were based on the *Model Rules* established by the American Bar Association, Choice *A*, the jurisdiction would still be in charge of implementing and defining their own application of the rules. The federal government, Choice *C*, or associates at a law firm, Choice *D*, may not have the same amount of information or knowledge about the certain rules of a jurisdiction as the authorities of the jurisdiction themselves have.

2. A: The lawyers who bought and sold the information would be subjected to punishment for releasing information that could potentially hurt a client who was formerly represented by a lawyer at the firm. Additionally, any lawyer who assists another lawyer in committing an act that would be considered unscrupulous in the profession is subject to disciplinary action along with all parties involved, even if the attorney was unaware that what they were doing was wrong. The attorney in this situation should have asked about the nature behind the request and used their best judgment to refrain from helping commit an unscrupulous activity.

3. B: A lawyer is required to report any misconduct they see performed by another attorney, even if it is unrelated to a case they are working. In this instance, a lawyer is allowed to charge extra for services to clients as long as they are agreed upon and are not grossly excessive to what would be reasonable. But if a lawyer is charging a client for services they have not performed, they are breaking their contract by lying to the client and stealing their money for nothing in return, and this should be reported. Choice *A*, only two times the normal amount, would probably not constitute enough of an upcharge to warrant misconduct charges.

4. D: Only a licensed lawyer for the state can practice law. Choice *A* is incorrect because the paralegal would be practicing law without a license. A paralegal cannot give clients information about how they should act in a situation relating to their case, making Choice *B* incorrect. Choice *C* is incorrect because any confidential information about a case is not to be shared with another attorney who is not part of the dispute.

5. C: A lawyer can only work in another state if they are certified by that state's board. Therefore, Choice *A* is incorrect. Choice *B* is incorrect because there are still exceptions to the rule, including working with and participating with an attorney who does work in that jurisdiction. Choice *D* is incorrect because marriage or any type of relationship does not have the power to transfer individual credentials in the law profession.

6. C: Legal fees are not permitted to be distributed to anyone who is not a lawyer working on the case. This includes an attorney's legal team, Choices *A* and *B*; their work is to be paid through regular compensations agreed upon at the time of hiring. The local jurisdictional authority, Choice *D*, would only be able to enforce this rule and would not allow the attorney to share legal funds received from a client.

7. B: Even if instructed by a superior, anyone in the law profession is required to follow ethical standards and not be a part of any action that could be considered misconduct. Following orders in this case would result in releasing confidential information that could be used against a client, making Choice *A* incorrect. Choice *C* is incorrect because the act may still go unreported, and Choice *D* is incorrect

because confidential information, regardless of the importance, would still be disclosed without a client and their lawyer's consent.

Domain II: The Client-Lawyer Relationship

8. B: The moment a party becomes a prospective client by speaking with a lawyer, their information becomes confidential. The information is not considered confidential if the individual is simply inquiring about representation, Choice *A*. However, if the case is discussed with a lawyer for prospective help, even prior to any contract, Choices *C* and *D*, the lawyer-client relationship is established, and all information related to the case should be kept confidential if spoken only between the lawyer and the person they could be representing.

9. D: If a lawyer feels they cannot complete their agreement, they need to compensate the client for time wasted and/or by finding a different attorney within a reasonable amount of time. A lawyer can limit their scope of representation without the approval of the jurisdiction, Choices *A* and *C*, but they need to do so before a contract is formed and an agreement is made between the client and the lawyer. The lawyer is required to commit to the terms agreed upon before starting a case, even if they do not charge fees, Choice *B*, so the client has a clear understanding of what will be accomplished.

10. D: The decision to have a trial by jury is an instance of actual authority, not apparent authority. This means only the client can make this type of decision, no matter the situation or timing. Just like deciding between a guilty and innocent plea, the attorney can inform the client of the possible outcomes of their decision, but the ultimate choice must be made by the client in any circumstance of actual authority.

11. A: As long as the lawyer is not committing to taking part in illegal activities or providing the client with information as to how they can get away with crimes, the lawyer is allowed to detail information about possible consequences of illegal actions. A contract, Choice *D*, also does not have to be written and signed when discussions are taking place, although information that is exchanged still needs to be kept confidential.

12. A: An attorney is not permitted to leave a client if it will cause hardships for them, especially if the trial date is approaching and a large amount of work has already been put into the case. However, there are situations that would permit the attorney to annul the relationship. If the attorney is fearful at any time because the client has acted violently toward them and poses a threat to their safety, they can end the lawyer-client relationship. The outburst that caused the client to put their hands on the attorney and push them down would be enough grounds for the lawyer to end their work with the client, even this close to a trial date, Choice *C*, and even though, in this situation, the lawyer was not seriously harmed, Choice *D*.

13. B: A contract can be established as soon as the lawyer-client relationship is formed. In this case, regardless of the method, the client still formed the relationship when they consulted the lawyer about their legal situation. A lawyer is not permitted to just ask for payment of services for a price that was not first discussed, Choice *A*. However, even though a contract does not need to be put in writing to be official, Choice *C*, if work is completed after a fee agreement has been made, Choice *D*, the client must pay the for services rendered for their case when they are billed or face legal consequences.

14. C: In the situation of staffing, the lawyer has the ultimate decision about how to run their firm or team. The lawyer is required to defer judgment to their clients on specific matters related to the outcome of their case. Not all decisions can be referred to in a contract; therefore, the number of staff

members an attorney employs is generally not stated because, although the attorney works for the client, the employees work under the attorney, making them the lawyer's responsibility.

15. D: Contingency fees are not allowed to be charged to clients who are facing criminal charges. The lawyer in this situation would have to ask for a flat fee or an hourly rate to be paid for their services, and if a contract was already formed, it needs to be annulled and changed to remove the contingency.

Domain III: Client Confidentiality
16. D: Even though the lawyer and the client had a conversation that would regularly be considered a consultation (establishing a lawyer-client relationship and protecting the information exchanged by attorney-client privilege), the conversation took place while the attorney was off work and at a party, not while they were practicing law. Therefore, the information exchanged is not legally confidential until it is discussed in a formal manner while the lawyer is at work and practicing.

17. A: If the prosecuting attorney can prove there is no other way to obtain the information acquired from the interview of the deceased person than through the other attorney's work-product document, the information would be required to be disclosed because it would have a significant effect on the outcome of the case. A lawyer's work documents are considered confidential in most cases and cannot be used by another attorney against someone's case, Choices *B* and *C*. No extra permissions would be needed by the prosecutor, Choice *D*.

18. A: If a third party is present and overhears information discussed between a lawyer and their client, the information is no longer considered confidential because it is not discussed solely between the two parties established in the contract. A friend of the client would hear the information, making it already subjected to disclosure. Choice *B*, a lawyer's notes, and Choice *D*, prospective client meetings, are considered confidential because they can contain important details a client may not want released. Choice *C* would also be confidential because the research could contain information the opposition could use as well, even though the lawyer may not have been involved in its creation.

19. A: The client has the power to make whatever decision they desire during a case, including disclosing confidential information, no matter how beneficial or harmful it might be to their situation. The lawyer is first and foremost responsible for acting out the requests made by the client at any time during a case.

20. B: An attorney is permitted to use any information or evidence they or their team created in defense about allegations brought against them, especially in this situation in which the client is claiming that not enough work was produced. The documents would also be allowed to be used regardless of whether the information they contain has confidential information, Choice *C*.

Domain IV: Conflicts of Interest
21. D: A lawyer is not allowed to give preference of time or materials to one client over another if they are representing multiple parties, putting them in a position where they are required to offer compensation to the party they have stopped representing as an end to any preference disputes. If the lawyer tries to rush one case, they are giving preference to the longer case, Choice *A*, and if they only work for the neediest client, Choice *B*, they are essentially abandoning the other. Meanwhile, they cannot simply hire more staff, as only a licensed lawyer is allowed to practice law and make a decision for a case, not a team of paralegals, Choice *C*.

80

22. B: As long as the lawyer does not in any way solicit or try to influence the donation of a gift, they are entitled to receive minor gifts. This is regardless of relation to the case, Choice *A*. Additionally, the stationary set is a minor gift, meaning it isn't of significant value, Choice *C*. The lawyer is permitted to accept the car because it was completely out of goodwill of the client, which does not have to be stated specifically in a contract, Choice *D*.

23. D: A client's confidential information remains confidential. This is true regardless of whether or not there is any relation between clients or cases, Choice *A*, and even after a case has ended, Choice *B*. An attorney can still represent clients who are related, Choice *C*, as long as their cases are not in opposition to each other, but information from past cases cannot be shared.

24. C: Any time a prospective client exchanges information with an attorney, the information needs to be kept confidential. Even though the contract was not finalized, Choice *B*, the attorney had already heard information that could be used against the party. This means they are barred from working any other case in which they might use this confidential information, especially including representing the opposing party. Prospective client information is treated the same as regular client information if spoken alone in confidence with a lawyer.

25. C: A law firm is never allowed to represent conflicting parties in a case, either past or present. Because the nature of the dispute was not personal and was directly related to the past case, the lawyer would not be permitted to represent the prospective client under these circumstances due to the imputed conflict. The fact that the two lawyers do not know each other, Choice *B*, is irrelevant; they both still work for the same firm, meaning they both could come in contact with confidential information that could harm the potential client's case.

26. C: A lawyer should not be motivated by anything other than their client's best interests. If the lawyer is interested in a case for the outcome of litigation, Choice *B*, rather than payment for representation, there would be a conflict of interest that would disallow the attorney from taking part in the case. A lawyer is free to market their services or approach a business or individual for representation, Choice *D*, but they must have no motives that could conflict with the requests of their clients.

27. B: In the case of contingency, the arrangement needs to be put in writing to avoid any disputes because the money is coming from the outcome of a case and not from a set dollar amount. The attorney is allowed to arrange their fees however they like as long as the client is in agreement with what fees should be paid for each service. This agreement can be verbal or written in the case of flat and hourly fees, Choice *A*.

28. D: If a client expects a third party to pay their legal fees, the third party needs to be informed and mentioned or written into a contract for all parties to agree to before they can be expected to pay. Therefore, Choice *A* is incorrect. The lawyer should not assume that another party will pay the bill for a client, Choice *B*, and cannot just send a bill to the business or unrelated party, Choice *C*. In this situation, the client would be the one responsible for the bill because they agreed to the contract for representation.

29. A: An attorney who worked as a government employee is restricted from representing a private client with a related case, even after they leave government employment. An attorney is permitted to represent family members if there are no personal conflicts with the opposing parties, Choice *B*. The

attorney can also represent a client any time after they obtain their license, Choice *C.* A lawyer can also work multiple, unrelated cases, Choice *D,* if they do not give preference to one client over the other.

Domain V: Competence, Legal Malpractice and Other Civil Liability

30. D: Although outsourcing certain types of work can help an attorney save time, it will not build upon the overall skill set or experience of the attorney in a way that will allow them to become and stay competent lawyers. Choice *A,* taking educational courses, and Choice *C,* attending a training seminar, can both help a lawyer learn new skills and gain knowledge about changing laws. Choice *B,* purchasing new software, will help the attorney ensure they are able to take advantage of technological updates to avoid falling behind other firms so they can stay competent in the law profession.

31. A: No specific qualifications are needed, other than being a licensed attorney in the jurisdiction, to take on a standard case that is taught extensively in school, such as a divorce hearing, especially if the attorney is already familiar with the proceedings in some capacity. As long as the client is aware that the attorney lacks experience, it would be at the client's discretion to decide whether they want to hire an inexperienced lawyer or not. Therefore, Choices *C* and *D* are incorrect. Choice *B* is incorrect because the attorney would not need to ask the jurisdiction in order to represent the client.

32. A: A diligent lawyer ensures that their client understands the consequences of their actions, including preventing them from unknowingly acting in a way that could hurt their case. Choice *B* is incorrect because there is no proof that the attorney did not gather enough evidence. Even though the specific instance of releasing the information may not have been the ultimate reason the case was lost, it was a contributing factor that could have been prevented. The client might have still decided to release the information, but at least the attorney would have shown diligence and care to inform the client of what the action could mean instead of simply following orders. Therefore, Choices *C* and *D* are incorrect.

33. B: If an attorney's negligence causes monetary damages to a member of their client's organization, the attorney is subject to civil liability from this party, regardless of whether the party is directly involved in the case or mentioned in the contract. Therefore, Choices *C* and *D* are incorrect. The board member was a nonclient, not an indirect client, making Choice *A* incorrect.

34. C: An attorney is not permitted to limit their liability for malpractice, even if the client agrees, because it would be considered an unethical attempt to take advantage of the client. Therefore, Choice *A* is incorrect. The client should not lose their right to hold the attorney accountable for malpractice simply because their case is considered to have a high chance of risk, making Choice *B* incorrect. An attorney can accept cases that carry more risk as long as they are qualified and the client's objectives are not considered unreasonable, making Choice *D* incorrect.

35. C: A lawyer is not allowed to try and limit their liability for malpractice in a contract, as it would be seen as unethical and a signifier of malicious intent rather than an attempt to fully represent the client according to the law. A lawyer is entitled to use all the methods at their disposal allowed by the law, including work product doctrine (Choice *A*), insurance (Choice *B*), and hiring additional attorneys to defend themselves against any malpractice claims (Choice *D*).

Domain VI: Litigation and Other Civil Liability

36. A: An attorney is permitted to accept cases the client may not know very much about because it is the attorney's job to gather the necessary evidence and information related to the case as they work.

Therefore, Choice *C* is incorrect. There is, however, an instance when an attorney might not be able to represent the client, and that is if there was a conflict of interest or the objectives were beyond the scope of the lawyer's capabilities, making Choice *B* incorrect. In this situation, gathering case evidence and trying to help the client is not beyond the scope of a licensed attorney, making Choice *D* also incorrect.

37. D: Even though the postponement will help the client's case, the client's request is still reasonable and the consequences were explained to the client, so the lawyer is obligated to do as their client demands and not postpone litigation. Therefore, Choice *A* is incorrect. Choice *B* is incorrect because time frames for goal completion do not need to be formally stated in a contract if discussed beforehand. The client's request would not create any unfair advantage, making Choice *C* also incorrect.

38. A: Under no circumstances should a lawyer fail to correct information they know is false, no matter how it might affect the client's position in a case. Therefore, Choice *C* is incorrect. Decisions made by the tribunal need to be based on factual information in order to be just decisions; it is up to the lawyer, client, and tribunal to ensure no false information is used during a case, making Choice *B* incorrect. Although most client requests need to be followed by the attorney, the client cannot forbid the lawyer from following the law and correcting a false statement, making Choice *D* incorrect.

39. A: An attorney is not responsible for disclosing every detail they or their team discover in a case, especially if the information might harm their chances of success or bear little outcome over the final verdict. Therefore, Choice *B* is incorrect. Because the lawyer is personally responsible for the orders given to their employees, in this case, the attorney would be subject to malpractice claims for instructing the hiding of evidence. Therefore, Choice *C* is incorrect. It also doesn't matter how important the evidence is or the outcome of the case, the attorney is never allowed to hide, destroy, or instruct their employees to hide or destroy any evidence, making Choice *D* also incorrect.

40. D: An attorney is allowed to discuss a case with a juror after they have been dismissed but not if the juror in any way expresses a desire to not speak with the attorney. Therefore, Choice *C* is incorrect. Although the discussion might help their client, no contract or agreement can be made that requires jurors to discuss case matters with any attorney after the trial has ended, making Choice *A* incorrect, and any expression to do so after the attorney has been initially denied (no matter how informally) must come from the juror, making Choice *B* also incorrect.

41. C: The ability to use persuasive argument with the evidence obtained in favor of the client is one of the most essential parts of practicing as an attorney. A lawyer can never make contractual agreements with a tribunal or judge, Choice *A*. They are also forbidden to have private discussion with jurors in which they could abuse their knowledge of legal proceedings, Choice *B*. Additionally, all evidence used in support of a client's case should be truthful and presented in a way that does not try to twist the facts, making Choice *D* incorrect.

42. B: An attorney is generally required to keep any information considered confidential from being disclosed to any outside party, especially if the client requests that the information be kept secret. Therefore, Choice *A* is incorrect. However, in matters in which the client may pose a threat to the public or people could be potentially harmed by a party involved in a criminal case, the attorney is required to disclose to the public any information that could keep people safe. They can disclose the information even if the client asked them not to, Choice *C,* or the information is considered confidential, Choice *D,*

83

because the client has been missing and has not contacted the attorney or informed them in any way of their decision to disappear.

43. B: An attorney cannot give testimony regarding personal experience in a case in which they are representing a client who has the financial means and time to find different representation, as it would cause a conflict of interest between the client's objectives and the attorney's ability to give all their evidence. A lawyer can give testimony regarding the scope and type of work they have performed for clients, even during trials in which they are representing one of the disputing parties, Choice *A*. They can also testify in trials they are not taking part in, even if an attorney who works in their firm is representing one of the parties involved, Choice *C*. If a client cannot afford to find new representation during a trial that a lawyer has evidence to give testimony for, the lawyer is still permitted to testify if allowed by the jurisdiction, Choice *D*.

Domain VII: Transactions and Communications with Persons Other Than Clients

44. A: In most cases, lawyers can choose to disclose or not disclose whatever they wish in order to help their client's case. They are expected to do what they legally can to win the case as long as they are not hiding or destroying evidence. They do not need the jurisdiction's approval first. Therefore, Choice *B* is incorrect. All parties should have a chance to discover the information, so it is not up to one attorney to disclose all the data they discover to the opposition, making Choice *C* incorrect. The client can decide to release the information, but the lawyer has no obligation to do so without a request, making Choice *D* also incorrect.

45. D: An attorney needs the expressed permission from the opposing attorney in order to have a discussion about the case between the two parties. This is to prevent the attorney from taking advantage of the opposing client without the knowledge of the opposing client's attorney.

Therefore, Choices *A*, *B*, and *C* are incorrect.

46. D: The attorney can only discuss a case with the opposing attorney in order to avoid an abuse of power or a client being taken advantage of. An opposing party (Choice *A*), an unrepresented party (Choice *B*), or even the local media (Choice *C*) have less of an understanding of the ethical uses of information relating to a case, and disclosing any information to them without the permission of the client could result in unwanted harm to their client. It also might be difficult to determine exactly what is common knowledge in the case and what is not, making it more of a possibility that confidential information may be accidently released if a discussion with other parties is undertaken. An opposing lawyer will know better what should or should not be discussed within the ethical guidelines of the jurisdiction.

Domain VIII: Different Roles of the Lawyer

47. B: A lawyer would never act as a juror on a trial because it might put them in a position to be biased against the tribunal and toward their client. A lawyer is expected to be an advisor for their client in order to provide diligent legal representation, making Choice *A* incorrect. They are also expected to be a negotiator during disputes in order to obtain a fair settlement for their client. Therefore, Choice *C* is incorrect. The lawyer is sometimes also asked to be an arbitrator for cases they are not representing a client in, making Choice *D* also incorrect.

48. C: If a lawyer is acting as a mediator, arbitrator, or any other third-party neutral for a case, they are relinquishing their responsibilities as an attorney and are expected to follow the ethical guidelines of

their position in the case. Choice *A* is incorrect because, although there isn't one, an opposing lawyer would have no authority over the decisions of the mediator in any case. Lawyers are not allowed to give counsel to any party, regardless of whether or not that party has representation, making Choice *B* incorrect. Whether acting as an arbitrator or mediator, the attorney should not provide any counsel or type of assistance, making Choice *D* incorrect.

49. D: The lawyer is permitted to go against the individual in this case because they are acting against the group's best interests in a way that could harm the case for the corporation. A corporation is made up of a large number of individuals; the attorney representing a corporation must decide what the interests of the group are as a whole over the individual agendas of even those chosen to represent the corporation. Therefore, Choice *A* is incorrect. The media is also not entitled to information related to the case, regardless of the client, making Choice *B* incorrect. Choice *C* is incorrect because confidential information can be disclosed if requested but only as long as revealing the information does not conflict with the goals of the group as a whole.

Domain IX: Safekeeping Funds and Other Property

50. C: Client funds must never be commingled with the attorney's funds for any length of time, no matter how temporary and even if it is meant to keep funds safe. Depositing the monies into the attorney's bank account, even temporarily to keep it safe until a trust account can be established (Choice *A*), is still a violation of the rules against the comingling of funds. Even if the secretary manages the practice and is trustworthy, Choice *B*, they must also be an authorized party able to create and deposit funds into a trust account in order to handle client funds. They cannot be considered a responsible party, Choice *D*, unless they are authorized to establish and access trust accounts.

51. A: When a dispute over trust account funds occurs, the attorney must hold the disputed funds in a joint account pending the resolution of the dispute. The attorney is not required to return disputed funds directly to the client, as indicated in Choice *B*. Choice *C* is incorrect because the attorney has no right to keep the money unless and until it is ruled so after the dispute is resolved. Choice *D* is incorrect because the client does have a right to dispute the disbursement of funds.

52. D: When an attorney takes possession of a client's property, the attorney must take care to properly identify and label the item, put the item in a secure location such as a safe deposit box, and notify all parties that the item is in the attorney's possession. Choice *A* is missing the requirement of identifying and labeling the property and instead it incorrectly states that the property must first be appraised before securing it and notifying parties. While California requires notification within fourteen days of receipt (as noted in Choice *B*), each state has its own requirements, and attorneys must follow the rules for their particular state. Choice *C* is correct once the case has been resolved, but this does not address the requirements attorneys must follow when assuming possession of the property in the first place.

Domain X: Communications about Legal Services

53. C: In the 1977 case of *Bates v. State Bar of Arizona*, the Supreme Court ruled that a total ban on attorney advertising represented a violation of their First Amendment rights. The Court also ruled that such advertising could be regulated. The case in Choice *A*, *Virginia Board of Pharmacists v. Virginia Citizens' Consumer Council*, established the groundwork for free speech in advertising with the ruling that the First Amendment protects free speech rights with regard to commercial speech. In Choice *B*, the case of *Alexander v. Cahill*, the court ruled that non-specific descriptive words were permissible in advertising. The case noted in Choice *D*, *Zauderer v. Office of Disciplinary Counsel*, established that the

requirement for attorneys to include their names and addresses in their advertising was not a violation of the freedom of commercial speech.

54. B: Including the names of clients without express written permission is a violation of the public communications rules for attorneys. The information in Choices *A*, *C*, and *D* is all included in the permitted twenty-five categories of information, so long as the information used is true, correct, and not misleading in any way.

55. A: The only way to solicit specific individuals who are known to have particular legal needs is via non-live, non-person-to-person contact, such as mailing a letter. This kind of contact can be easily disregarded by the person and thus does not constitute undue influence on the part of the attorney. All the other forms of contact in Choices *B*, *C*, and *D* are not permitted based on the idea that real time contact can prohibit the person from thinking about their choices and making informed decisions regarding their legal representation. Real time contact also allows for undue influence on the part of the attorney, which is a violation.

56. D: Once an agreement for a legal services program has been reached, anyone except the attorney and representatives of the law firm can contact the potential participants. In this case, the appropriate party would be the human resources department of the company. Choices *A* and *B* are both prohibited from soliciting employees' participation because they stand to enjoy monetary gain from the arrangement. Employees can be told about the program, however, making Choice *C* incorrect.

Domain XI: Lawyer's Duties to the Public and the Legal System

57. C: Attorneys may request excusal from an assignment based on undue financial burden. High-profile murders, for example, take a great deal of time and resources, and small, single-attorney practices are not often sufficiently equipped to handle them. While attorneys are permitted to request excusal for a lack of experience, as in Choice *B*, that is not the case in this example. Similarly, attorneys are not required to accept cases based on whether they have completed pro bono hours, Choice *A*, because pro bono hours can be met through other services beyond offering legal representation. Attorneys may not, however, request excusal from an assignment for just any reason, such as in Choice *D*.

Domain XII: Judicial Conduct

58. D: The Model Code of Judicial Conduct is a set of rules and guidelines that are specifically applicable to judges. The Model Rules of Professional Conduct, Choice *A*, are the governing rules and guidelines for attorneys and legal professionals. Choices *B* and *C* are made-up answers.

59. B: Judges may use their letterhead and title when writing a letter of recommendation so long as the judge has personal knowledge of the person and does not include anything that could be misconstrued as carrying judicial weight or influence. These situations are addressed in the Model Code of Judicial Conduct, Choice *A*, but the code does not expressly prohibit the use of the letterhead in total, Choice *C*. Additionally, judges are permitted to write letters of recommendation in their professional capacity, Choice *D*, so long as they are done so appropriately.

60. C: When a judge inadvertently receives an ex parte communication, both parties in the case must be notified of the contents of the communication and given an opportunity to respond. The communication cannot simply be ignored, Choice *A*, as the judge having knowledge about one side over the other could materially affect the case. Similarly, the judge cannot simply share the communication, Choice *B*, without first addressing the situation with both parties. Recusal, Choice *D*, is not necessary.

Practice Test #2

Domain I: Regulation of the Legal Profession

1. A bar applicant asks an attorney to provide an affidavit of her good character for her bar application. The applicant is the niece of one of the attorney's partners in their firm. The attorney has known the applicant for over 10 years but did not work with her in a legal context while she was an intern at their firm. The attorney reasonably believes that the applicant possesses good character and thus provides an affidavit.

Is the attorney subject to discipline for providing the affidavit?
   a. Yes, because the applicant is a family member of one of the firm's partners.
   b. Yes, because the attorney did not personally work with the applicant in a legal context.
   c. No, because an affidavit of good character does not require legal knowledge.
   d. No, because the applicant does not belong to the partner's immediate household.

2. During a civil case, the plaintiff's attorney is contacted by the defendant's lawyer. The lawyer presents an offer to settle the case. The settlement is given in writing but is not signed by the defendant. The attorney inquires about this, and the lawyer explains that they are offering this settlement because it's in their client's best interest.

The attorney declines the settlement offer. Is the plaintiff's attorney obligated to report this situation to an appropriate authority?
   a. Yes, because the defendant's lawyer didn't reasonably believe they were acting in their client's best interest.
   b. Yes, because the attorney reasonably believes the defendant was not informed of the settlement offer by their lawyer.
   c. No, because this occurred during a civil case, not a criminal case.
   d. No, because the defendant's lawyer was reasonably acting in their client's best interest.

3. An attorney who practices in Florida has a client who becomes involved in a civil suit in Georgia. Due to their existing relationship, the client wants the attorney to advise them during the case. The attorney agrees, provided that a lawyer practicing in Georgia is also on the legal team. Subsequently, the client also hires a Georgian lawyer for this suit. The local jurisdiction has no statutes with special restrictions on who can work in the county.

Is the attorney subject to discipline for working this suit?
   a. Yes, because the attorney is practicing law outside the state in which they are licensed.
   b. Yes, because their existing relationship means the attorney should not have required the client to hire a local lawyer.
   c. No, because the local jurisdiction allows anyone who practices law to practice within the county.
   d. No, because the attorney will be working in association with a lawyer licensed to practice in Georgia.

4. A woman comes to an attorney seeking to reduce her alimony payments to her ex-husband. She is currently paying $2,000 per month. The prospective client offers to pay the attorney their standard fee as well as a bonus fee that would be contingent on the alimony payment being reduced to $1,000 per month or less. The attorney investigates the woman's finances as well as her ex-husband's finances, concludes that this goal of litigation is plausible, and accepts the case. After the trial, the woman's alimony payments are reduced to $750 per month. She pays the attorney the bonus fee, as agreed. Has the attorney engaged in misconduct?

 a. No, because the attorney is following the initial agreement made with the client.
 b. No, because the attorney investigated both parties' finances prior to accepting the case.
 c. Yes, because the attorney was already in a client-lawyer relationship with the ex-husband.
 d. Yes, because the attorney accepted a bonus fee contingent on the reduction of the alimony.

5. An attorney's client has the goal of winning as large a settlement as possible in a domestic dispute case. One day, the client tells their attorney that the opposing party has made them an offer to settle the dispute and concede to all the client's demands provided that the attorney promises to never bring another case against the conceding party. What would be the BEST course of action for the lawyer to take to represent the client's best interests in this situation?

 a. Accept the deal to achieve the client's goal
 b. Make a counteroffer that includes the promise that no cases will be brought against either client as well
 c. Decline the offer
 d. Withdraw from representation for ethical reasons

Domain II: The Client-Lawyer Relationship

6. An attorney charges $200 per hour for their services in civil proceedings. Three other lawyers in the same city charge $220, $150, and $190, respectively. In a larger city an hour and a half away, most lawyers charge their clients $500 per hour when working a civil suit.
Would it constitute misconduct if the attorney increased their fee to $400 per hour?

 a. Yes, because the attorney is charging an unreasonable fee for their locality.
 b. Yes, because the attorney didn't formally consult with their legal colleagues about the change.
 c. No, because the attorney is charging less than lawyers in the nearby city.
 d. No, because the attorney's fee is considered reasonable for their locality.

7. An attorney's client is suing their former employer, a national retail corporation. The client alleges that the former employer denied reasonable accommodations for the client's disability and then fired the client without just cause. The client confides that their objective is to get an acceptable settlement quickly in order to pay their bills. However, the attorney believes they can win a substantially larger award in a trial, which may require waiting several years.
The former employer's legal team sends the attorney a settlement offer for lower than the client's goal. The attorney rejects the offer immediately because they believe a trial is in the best interest of their client.
Is the attorney subject to discipline?

 a. Yes, because their client was willing to accept any settlement for a quick resolution of the suit.
 b. Yes, because the attorney did not abide by the client's stated objectives for the case.
 c. No, because the attorney was acting in the client's best interest in rejecting the settlement.
 d. No, because rejecting the settlement offer was implicitly within the scope of the attorney's authority in representing the client.

88

8. An attorney is retained by the legal team of a local factory as an expert in environmental law. The factory's leadership team tasks the attorney with investigating the factory's current waste management practices. The attorney finds that the factory's current practices are in violation of state regulations, and she reports this to the legal team along with her findings. Later, the attorney learns that the leadership team used this information to conceal overt signs of the factory's inadequate waste management system. The attorney contacted the legal team to inform them that she would be terminating her relationship with the factory.

Is this attorney subject to discipline?
    a. Yes, because the attorney did not act in the client's best interest in terminating the relationship.
    b. Yes, because the attorney reported violations to the factory instead of immediately informing a local authority.
    c. No, because the leadership team used the attorney's work in an attempt to evade regulatory requirements.
    d. No, because the client had no obligation to remain in a client-lawyer relationship after receiving the report.

9. An established client meets with an attorney to discuss the insurance for their office building. During the conversation, the client initiates a discussion about what would happen if the building were to burn down. They joke that the insurance claim would provide more revenue than the client makes from operating the building. They also joke that the attorney's fee for resolving such an insurance claim would be a lot of money. The client then emphasizes that they are describing a hypothetical situation.

Is the attorney obligated to terminate their relationship with this client?
    a. Yes, because the client's jokes provide reasonable evidence that they plan to commit insurance fraud.
    b. Yes, because an attorney is not permitted to discuss hypothetical situations such as this with a client.
    c. No, because the attorney can reasonably conclude that the client is joking rather than being serious.
    d. No, because the client is not directly asking the attorney to help them commit fraud.

10. An attorney is named as the executor of a client's will. The client has passed away, and the will does not specify when and where it shall be read to the client's heirs. Acting as executor, the attorney decides that it will be read one hour after the funeral in a conference room at the client's church, which hosted the wake and the funeral.

One of the client's children is not named as a beneficiary of the will. Prior to the funeral, that child reports that they are unable to attend the funeral. That child also contests that the time and location of reading the will is impermissible since they will not be able to attend.

Did the attorney act outside their authority in this situation?
    a. No, because the time and location of reading the will were not specified.
    b. No, because as executor, the attorney had authority delegated to them by the deceased client.
    c. Yes, because the attorney did not have explicit authority to determine when and where the will would be read.
    d. Yes, because the child had actual authority to insist on being able to be present when the will was read.

11. During a Fourth of July celebration, a person expresses frustration that fireworks set off by one of their neighbors damaged their house. An attorney offers their services to the person if they choose to seek legal action. The person declines and politely informs the attorney that they aren't currently interested in retaining legal services.

Two weeks later, the lawyer sends the person an email to remind them of the offer. The lawyer further offers to take the case *pro bono* as a sign of goodwill.

Is this attorney's email solicitation considered misconduct?

    a. Yes, because they are soliciting an individual who has expressed a desire not to receive further solicitation.

    b. Yes, because it is unprofessional for an attorney to offer to do *pro bono* work for a prospective client.

    c. No, because the attorney is not seeking pecuniary gain from the solicitation.

    d. No, because the attorney reasonably believes that the person would form a client-lawyer relationship if they did not have to pay the lawyer's fees.

12. An attorney is contacted by the manager of a local ball bearings factory. Five years ago, the attorney was the plaintiffs' lawyer in a class action lawsuit by the factory's employees. The employees won the case and received compensation from the factory for unpaid wages.

The current manager did not work for the factory during that case. The manager asks the attorney to represent the factory in a new lawsuit. The new case is a claim for workers' compensation following an employee's injury during work at the factory. The employee was a member of the class action suit. No other members of the class action suit are involved in the case, so the attorney agrees to represent the factory.

Is the attorney subject to discipline for this decision?

    a. Yes, because the attorney has a duty to their former clients not to represent the factory in any capacity.

    b. Yes, because the attorney has a duty to the suing employee not to represent the factory in related cases.

    c. No, because the attorney does not have a duty to a former client since the prior case was a class action lawsuit.

    d. No, because the manager is a prospective client who was not involved in this employee's prior lawsuit.

13. An attorney is representing the defendant in a criminal case for theft. The attorney and the client discuss a plea bargain but are unable to reach an agreement with the prosecution. The case goes to trial. At the beginning of the trial, the client asks the attorney how long the trial will take. The attorney says "three months" but emphasizes that this is a guess that they can't guarantee. After 14 weeks, the trial continues to be ongoing. The client emails the attorney on a Wednesday asking how much longer the trial will take. The attorney responds that they are not sure and offers to discuss the matter when they meet on the following Monday.

Is this attorney's email communication with the client considered misconduct?
   a. Yes, because the attorney failed in their obligation to comply with a client's reasonable request for information.
   b. Yes, because the attorney should not have waited until the following Monday to give their client a complete answer.
   c. No, because the attorney had already answered this question at the beginning of the trial.
   d. No, because this question does not constitute a reasonable request for information by the client.

Domain III: Client Confidentiality

14. An attorney is representing a major retail corporation as the defendant in a class action lawsuit. The client is considering a settlement and sends the settlement offer to the attorney and other members of the legal team. The next day, the drafted settlement offer is made public by a news station. The corporation did not approve the release of this document, and the attorney was not responsible for releasing it.

Later that evening, one of the attorney's colleagues asks for the attorney's opinion on the drafted settlement offer.

Is the document still protected by attorney-client privilege?
   a. Yes, because the document was not made public by an authorized representative of the client.
   b. Yes, because all matters concerning the case are protected until the case is resolved.
   c. No, because once such a document is made public, it is no longer considered confidential.
   d. No, because if the document was sent only to authorized representatives, it must have been provided to the news station with the client's permission.

15. An attorney is representing the defense in a criminal trial for attempted murder. Their client is accused of attempting to murder her ex-boyfriend. The jury acquits the defendant of the charges. After the trial, the client privately confesses to the attorney that she did attempt to murder her ex-boyfriend. She expresses the desire to attempt the murder again at some point in the future but does not specify the method by which she would do so.

Hearing this, the attorney reports their client's future desire to commit murder to a local police authority.

Is the attorney subject to discipline for breaking confidentiality?
   a. Yes, because the client was acquitted, and her constitutional rights protect her from double jeopardy.
   b. Yes, because it is unreasonable for the attorney to believe the client would attempt to harm her ex-boyfriend since the client did not specify a method.
   c. No, because the attorney is obliged to report any information that is reasonably necessary to prevent bodily harm.
   d. No, because confidentiality is no longer expected since the defendant was acquitted and is now a former client of the attorney.

16. An attorney is representing a defendant in a criminal case. At the client's request, their religious authority has been included in all of the legal team's proceedings during the case. The attorney advises against this since the religious authority is not a legal professional. The client has signed a document consenting to the religious authority's receipt of confidential information related to the case. In accordance with the client's directions, the attorney includes the religious authority in all discussions about the case and sends them all documentation related to the case as they would another lawyer on the legal team.

During the trial, the religious authority withdraws from the client's team, makes public a document the attorney sent them, and states that the client is no longer welcome in their community.

Is the attorney subject to discipline?

    a. Yes, because the attorney shared confidential information with a person who does not belong to the legal profession.

    b. Yes, because the attorney sent a document to the religious authority that resulted in substantial emotional harm to the client.

    c. No, because a religious authority is not required to follow the same confidentiality requirements as a lawyer.

    d. No, because the client provided written consent to send all documentation concerning the case to the religious authority.

17. An attorney is defending a factory's manager in a criminal case regarding workplace safety. Two years before the trial, the client came to the attorney and expressed concerns about inadequate safety training in the workplace, which could result in litigation. The client reported that their attempts to implement training were repeatedly denied by the factory's CEO. The attorney advised the client to notarize an affidavit each time they were denied additional funds for training.

While preparing for the trial, the prosecution subpoenas the attorney requesting any documentation pertaining to the case. The attorney provides the prosecution with six notarized affidavits.

Is the attorney subject to discipline?

    a. Yes, because all conversations between the attorney and their client were protected by attorney-client privilege.

    b. Yes, because the affidavits were created in preparation for litigation and so are protected by the work-product doctrine.

    c. No, because the attorney was complying with a legal command to provide the documentation as part of the discovery process.

    d. No, because the affidavits were notarized and therefore are not considered confidential information.

18. An attorney is representing the plaintiff in a civil suit in Louisiana. The attorney calls the defendant's lawyer to schedule a time to meet and negotiate a proposed settlement offer. The plaintiff, who is not prohibited from traveling, is currently in Mississippi and will return to Louisiana in three days. The defendant's lawyer suggests meeting in two days. The attorney shares that their client is currently not in Louisiana but will return soon. They suggest meeting in four days. The defendant's lawyer agrees. Has the attorney disclosed confidential information to the defendant's lawyer?

    a.   Yes, because a client's location is confidential information that may not be shared without explicit written consent.

    b.   Yes, because a client's location is confidential information, and the attorney may reasonably believe they have implied consent to disclose it.

    c.   No, because a client's location is only considered confidential information if there is a substantial cause to believe that disclosing it will cause bodily harm.

    d.   No, because a client's location is only considered confidential information during a criminal suit.

Domain IV: Conflicts of Interest

19. An attorney has agreed to represent three construction companies jointly in a case seeking to overturn a new regulatory rule made by the city in which all three operate. Overturning this rule seems likely to benefit all three companies equally.

During the case, one of the company owners confides in the attorney that overturning the rule will allow their company to implement a major development project that this owner has been planning for several years. The owner further confides that they hope to dominate the local market after completing this project. They ask the attorney not to inform the other companies of this planned project. The attorney agrees not to do so.

Has the attorney engaged in misconduct?

    a.   Yes, because the attorney has an equal duty of loyalty to all three of the clients in this case.

    b.   Yes, because the attorney is obliged to share all information with all clients, even trade secrets.

    c.   No, because the company owner's statement is protected by attorney-client privilege as confidential information.

    d.   No, because the attorney is only obliged to share information that directly pertains to the case seeking to overturn the city's rule.

20. An established client is retiring and downsizing from their current lifestyle to a more modest lifestyle. They contact their attorney to ask for their assistance in legal matters when selling the client's business. The attorney agrees. While downsizing, the client offers to sell their house to the attorney. The attorney agrees to buy it for a fair market rate. The attorney advises the client to seek independent representation for this transaction and provides this advice in writing. The client acknowledges this and writes back that they consent to maintaining the client-lawyer relationship without additional representation. The attorney buys the house from the client. Is the attorney subject to discipline?

    a.   Yes, because the attorney completed an inappropriate business transaction with the client in buying the house.

    b.   Yes, because the attorney was obligated to recuse themselves from representing the client during the business transaction.

    c.   No, because the attorney was acting in the client's best interest by accepting the client's offer to sell the house.

    d.   No, because the attorney advised the client to seek independent representation and received their informed consent in writing.

21. In the past, an attorney represented the plaintiff in a suit against his employer for unpaid PTO upon being laid off. The attorney was privilege to information about the client's personal life, including his relationship with his spouse and their children. The attorney was aware of domestic troubles, but no activities violated legal or ethical boundaries.

The former client's spouse approaches the attorney seeking representation to divorce the former client. The attorney agrees. During the divorce proceedings, the attorney does not disclose information provided by the former client about the couple's domestic life during the prior lawsuit. All information used in the divorce case is provided by the former client's spouse. The spouse divorces the former client with a favorable alimony and child support settlement.

Is this attorney subject to discipline?
- a. Yes, because the attorney, in withholding information, did not act in their current client's best interest.
- b. Yes, because the attorney formed a client-lawyer relationship with someone whose interests were materially adverse to the former client.
- c. No, because the divorce case is not substantially similar to the case in which the attorney represented their former client.
- d. No, because the attorney successfully achieved the spouse's objectives in seeking representation.

22. An attorney works at a firm that specializes in personal injury law. The attorney is contacted by the legal team of a wealthy individual who was recently in a car accident. Another person involved in the car accident is suing the prospective client for medical expenses not covered by insurance. The legal team asks the attorney to testify against the plaintiff as an expert in personal injury law in exchange for a fee. The plaintiff is currently represented by another lawyer who works at the attorney's firm. The attorney does not have a personal relationship with that lawyer. The attorney is not otherwise involved in the case and has never formed a client-lawyer relationship with the plaintiff. The attorney agrees to testify for the defendant.

Does this constitute misconduct?
- a. Yes, because the attorney is associated with the firm that is representing the plaintiff in this case.
- b. Yes, because working at this firm doesn't logically necessitate that the attorney is actually an expert in personal injury law.
- c. No, because the attorney's relationships are not restricted by their colleague's relationship with the plaintiff.
- d. No, because accepting a fee for expert testimony does not constitute representing a client whose interests are adverse to the plaintiff.

23. An attorney who specializes in labor relations is contacted by an employee of a major retail chain. The employee wants to sue the retail chain for illegal union-busting activities. The employee provides internal documentation that the attorney reasonably believes provides evidence of collusion or conspiracy.

The attorney's stock portfolio includes holdings in the retail chain. The attorney purchased these stocks over five years ago. The attorney's stock does not provide them with a substantially influential say in corporate policy or activities. The attorney takes the employee's case and successfully sues the retail chain. The attorney does not sell their holdings in the retail chain during or after this lawsuit.

Has this attorney engaged in misconduct?

    a. No, because the attorney did not use their knowledge of the lawsuit to engage in insider trading by selling their stocks.

    b. No, because it is reasonably certain that the attorney acted with full competence because they won the case, despite a potential financial harm to the attorney.

    c. Yes, because as a stockholder, the attorney had an obligation to inform the retail chain of the employee's lawsuit.

    d. Yes, because the attorney did not secure the employee's informed consent about the attorney's material interest in the corporation.

24. An attorney is representing a construction company that is seeking to purchase one of its competitors. The government has filed an antitrust suit to investigate whether or not this merger would constitute a regional monopoly. The attorney reasonably believes that this will not constitute a monopoly due to the presence of other companies in the region. During the course of the suit, the company's CEO describes to the attorney how they hope to expand the company's projects into new housing developments.

While representing the construction company, the attorney purchases undeveloped land in the geographical areas the CEO expressed interest in developing. The attorney's case is successful, and the client company purchases its competitor. The attorney then sells the land to their former client for a profit.

Is the attorney subject to discipline?

    a. Yes, because they acquired a pecuniary interest in the outcome of the case.

    b. Yes, because they did not disclose the CEO's plans to an authority as evidence that the company is seeking to establish a regional monopoly.

    c. No, because they sold the undeveloped land to their former client, thus acting in the client's interest.

    d. No, because purchasing land is not reasonably considered to be associated with the client's case.

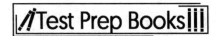

25. A judge assumes the role of a neutral mediator between two husbands during a divorce. One of the men is represented by a lawyer, and the other is not. The judge informs both men that she is not a representative for either party. The judge informs them of the fee for mediation, and both parties agree. Both parties are unwilling to agree to the results of mediation, so the divorce goes to trial. The judge is not involved in the trial.

The unrepresented husband contacts the judge and asks her to represent him as a lawyer during the divorce case. The judge declines. After the trial has concluded, the judge has not received compensation for her mediation. She files a suit requesting the agreed-upon fee from both parties.

Is this judge subject to discipline?

    a. Yes, because the judge ought to have agreed to represent the unrepresented party because as mediator, she had established a client-lawyer relationship.

    b. Yes, because as a third-party neutral, the judge was not permitted to file a suit to receive her fee.

    c. No, because the judge appropriately avoided forming a client-lawyer relationship with either of the men.

    d. No, because the judge was not involved in the divorce proceedings and so had the freedom to choose whether or not to take the man as a client.

26. A law clerk is working with the judge on a criminal case for sexual assault. While acting in this capacity, the law clerk is seeking employment with law firms in the same city and informs the judge that they are seeking employment as an attorney. During the case, the law clerk is contacted by a lawyer who works at the same firm as the defendant's representation. The lawyer makes an offer of employment to the law clerk. The law clerk informs the judge that they will be leaving the case and accepts the offer of employment.

Is the law clerk subject to discipline?

    a. Yes, because they are substantially involved in a case in which the lawyer's firm is representing the defendant.

    b. Yes, because the law clerk should not have sought employment while involved in a criminal case.

    c. No, because the lawyer is responsible for having made an inappropriate offer of employment to the law clerk.

    d. No, because the law clerk satisfied their obligations by informing the judge that they were seeking employment.

27. A lawyer who was once an arbitrator for a divorce settlement is later asked by one of the parties in the dispute to represent them in an appeal. The opposing party is contacted about the arrangement and states that they do not mind if the lawyer represents the client even though the lawyer might still have access to confidential information related to the divorce settlement. Is the lawyer permitted to represent the client?

    a. Yes, as long as both parties agree.

    b. Yes, as long as the attorney keeps all information from the previous case that could be used against the opposition confidential.

    c. No, because the attorney is never permitted to represent a party that was involved in a previous case in which the attorney acted as a mediator or judge.

    d. Yes, as long as all parties sign a written agreement.

Domain V: Competence, Legal Malpractice, and Other Civil Liability

28. An attorney takes on a new client who is suing their employer for unpaid wages owed at the time of termination. During the attorney's investigation of the evidence to prepare for the case, the local statute of limitations for such a suit expires. The suit can no longer be filed against the employer.

The attorney's malpractice insurance states that the attorney must report all potential malpractice claims within 30 days; otherwise, the attorney will be liable for the claim. The client responds in writing to the attorney that they do not intend to sue for malpractice. The attorney does not report the potential malpractice claim to their insurance.

If the client brings a suit, will the attorney be covered by their malpractice insurance?
   a. Yes, because they have written documentation that the client settled the claim without litigation.
   b. Yes, because the client has waived their right to a malpractice suit for this case.
   c. No, because the attorney did not report the potential malpractice claim to their insurance provider.
   d. No, because the attorney is not liable for malpractice because they worked with appropriate diligence.

29. An attorney is exploring the utility of new artificial intelligence (AI) technologies to maintain their competence in the field of digital copyright law. During a civil case, the attorney uses an AI program to generate the text of their closing argument. The attorney provides the program with all relevant information about the case. The attorney gives the closing argument as written by the AI program. After deliberation, the attorney's client wins the case.

Is the attorney subject to discipline for using this technology?
   a. Yes, because the attorney did not write the closing argument themselves.
   b. Yes, because the attorney utilized technology that they were not competent in during an actual court case.
   c. No, because the attorney appropriately determined a method by which to become competent with the new technology.
   d. No, because using an AI program is relevant to the attorney's field of expertise.

30. An attorney has retired but has maintained their client-lawyer relationships with two clients due to the longevity of these particular relationships. The attorney contacts their former firm and requests the services of a lawyer to assist their clients in case of the attorney's illness or death. The attorney drafts a document assigning their clients' files to a younger lawyer at their former firm in that circumstance. Then, the attorney provides the document to both of their clients. Both clients agree to the plan and sign the document.

Has the attorney shown due diligence to their clients?
   a. Yes, because the attorney ensured both clients consented to the attorney's plan in case of the attorney's death or disability.
   b. Yes, because the attorney ensured their client-lawyer relationships would continue even after the attorney retired.
   c. No, because the attorney ought to have recommended the clients form a relationship with a new lawyer.
   d. No, because the attorney contacted their former firm instead of seeking out the best possible lawyer to designate in the plan.

31. A tribunal appoints an attorney to represent the defendant in a criminal case. The victims in this case were children. The attorney is a parent and a grandparent. The attorney declines the appointment on the grounds that the alleged crimes are so repugnant that the attorney does not believe they will be able to provide competent legal representation.

Is the attorney liable for malpractice due to incompetence?
   a. Yes, because a competent lawyer is reasonably expected to provide representation in such a case despite bias.
   b. Yes, because the attorney is obliged to accept the tribunal's appointment even if they consider the cause to be repugnant.
   c. No, because the attorney reasonably argued that they would be incapable of providing competent representation.
   d. No, because the attorney's competence is not logically associated with their ability to provide the defendant with representation.

32. An employee is suing their employer following a workplace injury. An attorney accepts the case representing the defendant. When drafting the agreement documenting their client-lawyer relationship, the attorney adds a malpractice liability section. This section states that the attorney is not liable for a malpractice suit if the plaintiff wins the case, if the attorney overlooks available information during the case, or if the case results in a class action lawsuit against the employer. The client is informed about these conditions and signs the agreement.

During the trial, the attorney's representation is competent and shows due diligence. There is no cause for a malpractice suit during the trial. The plaintiff wins the case.

Were the attorney's malpractice liability stipulations appropriate?
   a. Yes, because losing a case does not necessarily indicate that a lawyer lacked competence.
   b. Yes, because the client was willing to give informed consent to these stipulations.
   c. No, because the attorney could still be held liable if the case were to become a class action lawsuit.
   d. No, because it is considered gross negligence for a lawyer to overlook relevant information.

33. In the state of Minnesota, a lawyer is required to report their continuing education hours once every three years. They are required to accrue a total of forty-five hours. They must report a minimum of three ethics credit hours and two elimination of bias credit hours.

An attorney reports four hours of ethics education, one hour of elimination of bias education, and forty hours of additional continuing education. This is the entirety of the attorney's engagement with continuing education and licensing.

Is the attorney still considered competent to practice law in Minnesota?
   a. Yes, because the attorney has completed the required forty-five hours of continuing education.
   b. Yes, because a lawyer is only considered incompetent if they've been found subject to discipline due to malpractice.
   c. No, because the attorney has not renewed their license to practice law.
   d. No, because the attorney has not completed the requisite hours of ethics education.

Domain VI: Litigation and Other Forms of Advocacy

34. An attorney is representing the defendant in a criminal case. The trial is almost complete, and the client asks the attorney to delay it for one week. The client explains that their child's birthday is next week and that they want to ensure they'll be able to attend. The client fears they'll be found guilty and will be sentenced to prison.

The attorney agrees to delay the trial. When the next trial date is scheduled, the attorney reports a conflict with another case. The trial is postponed until after the child's birthday. The client attends the day of the trial and is found guilty.

Is the attorney subject to discipline for delaying the trial?
   a. Yes, because they did not fulfill their duty to expedite the litigation.
   b. Yes, because the attorney delayed the trial to help their client avoid being found guilty.
   c. No, because the attorney had reasonable cause for delaying the litigation.
   d. No, because the attorney was acting to complete their client's strategic objectives.

35. An attorney is representing the defendant in a civil case. The defendant is an employee accused of stealing by reporting inaccurate working hours. The attorney has private knowledge that the defendant did lie about their hours. During discovery, the attorney finds that the employer has video evidence of their client arriving at one time but recording a different time. The video evidence comes from a visible security camera watching the building's front door from across the street.

The attorney files a motion to suppress the video evidence, asserting that the defendant did not consent to being filmed by the employer. The motion is dismissed by the judge.

Was the attorney obligated to file this motion?
   a. Yes, because the attorney is obligated to contest the opposition's evidence whenever a reasonable cause can be claimed.
   b. Yes, because the attorney is asserting the defendant's right to consent to workplace surveillance.
   c. No, because the attorney is not obligated to file frivolous motions even if they would benefit the client.
   d. No, because the attorney's obligations to represent the client do not extend to contesting the plaintiff's evidence.

36. An attorney is prosecuting a criminal theft case. One of the defense's witnesses is testifying about a time over a decade ago when the defendant returned lost property rather than stealing it. The attorney makes an objection that the testimony is not relevant because the lost property was not valuable. The judge denies the objection.

After the session, the defense lawyer expresses frustration at the frequency of the attorney's objections. The attorney and the lawyer shake hands and depart amicably.

Was the attorney's objection frivolous?
   a. No, because the objection was not made with the intent to frustrate the opposition.
   b. No, because the attorney objected to the testimony reasonably believing it was not relevant.
   c. Yes, because the testimony is reasonably relevant to a case prosecuting theft.
   d. Yes, because the attorney is likely making more objections than is professionally appropriate.

99

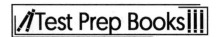

37. An attorney meets with a judge for an *ex parte* proceeding to consider a temporary restraining order. The attorney represents the husband in the related divorce case. The husband is seeking a restraining order on the wife due to domestic violence. The wife's representation is not present. During the proceeding, the attorney presents the husband's argument for a temporary restraining order. The attorney also describes why they reasonably believe the husband's request is necessary. When the judge asks if there is any reason they shouldn't approve a temporary restraining order, the attorney describes the merits of continued contact for coordinating childcare for the divorcing couple's children. The temporary restraining order is denied.
Is the attorney subject to discipline?
   a. Yes, because the attorney did not act in their client's best interest during the proceeding.
   b. Yes, because the attorney did not insist on both parties having representation at the proceeding.
   c. No, because the attorney had an obligation to help the judge make an informed decision.
   d. No, because the attorney successfully advocated for their client's interests to the judge.

38. An attorney is representing a local public official accused of embezzling government funds. During the discovery prior to a trial for this allegation, the attorney is confronted by a newspaper reporter. The reporter asks for information about the case. The attorney states that the official has been accused of embezzling and that a trial date has not yet been determined.
Is the attorney subject to discipline?
   a. No, because the attorney provided the reporter with publicly available information.
   b. No, because the attorney is not obliged to conceal the truth when speaking with the press.
   c. Yes, because the attorney may only speak with members of the public about a case during an official press conference.
   d. Yes, because the attorney confirmed for the reporter that their client was accused of embezzling.

39. An attorney's child is accused of theft, and the attorney decides to act as their representation. During the trial, the attorney is called to testify by the prosecution. The attorney testifies that their child was at home on the evening of the theft. Later, the prosecution calls a witness who testifies that the child was seen that evening out of the home.
Has the attorney engaged in misconduct?
   a. Yes, because they should not have testified against their client.
   b. Yes, because they should not have decided to represent the client in this case.
   c. No, because the attorney could have reasonably believed that the client was at home.
   d. No, because the attorney has fulfilled their legal requirement to tell the truth while under oath.

Domain VII: Transactions and Communications with Persons Other Than Clients

40. An attorney is representing Jen, one of three plaintiffs in a civil case. All three plaintiffs are employees of a local independent retail store. They each have individual legal representation and are suing the store for damages due to harassment by a manager.

One of the other plaintiffs, Harry, was recently injured in a car accident for which he was not at fault. Harry's insurance has not paid the full claim owed under his personal injury protection policy. He has not yet secured legal representation for this personal injury case. Harry asks Jen's attorney for advice on how to get paid. The attorney advises that they are not an expert on personal injury law, and the attorney gives Harry a recommendation for a personal injury lawyer.

Is the attorney subject to discipline?

a. Yes, because the attorney gave Harry legal advice while he was already represented by another lawyer during the civil case.

b. Yes, because the attorney neglected their obligations to Jen by giving this recommendation to Harry.

c. No, because the attorney is reasonably able to advise both Jen and Harry since they're plaintiffs in the same lawsuit.

d. No, because the attorney's advice is unrelated to the subject for which Harry is already represented.

41. An attorney is representing a client during the appeals process after a tax audit. During this process, the client gives the attorney a USB flash drive that contains the client's financial documents and other personal information. While examining the contents of this drive to prepare for the appeal, the attorney discovers a folder of private correspondence and photographs that do not pertain to the tax case. However, they do provide information concerning the client's business partner, who is also one of the attorney's clients in a civil case regarding property zoning.

The next meeting between the attorney and the client is two weeks later. The attorney returns the drive to the client and informs the client that the attorney had access to their business partner's personal information while using the drive in the normal course of the attorney's legal duties.

Has the attorney engaged in misconduct?

a. Yes, because the attorney did not inform the business partner that the client inadvertently sent private correspondence to the attorney.

b. Yes, because the attorney waited two weeks before notifying the client of the documents that were inadvertently included on the drive.

c. No, because the attorney informed the client at an appropriate time and in an appropriate manner.

d. No, because the attorney reasonably believed that the business partner had consented to sharing these documents since the attorney represented both individuals.

Domain VIII: Different Roles of the Lawyer

42. An attorney is representing a husband during a divorce case. The couple agree to try arbitration with a judge rather than taking the case to court. During arbitration, the attorney reports to the judge that the couple's house is worth about $300,000. The wife's lawyer agrees that they believe this estimate to be reasonably accurate. While dividing the couple's assets, the judge awards the house to the husband. After the divorce is finalized, the husband sells the house and reports to the attorney that the house sold for $450,000. The attorney congratulates their client on the sale.
Is this attorney subject to discipline for dishonest conduct?
   a. Yes, because the house was sold for substantially more than the attorney estimated during arbitration.
   b. Yes, because the attorney did not inform the wife or her lawyer of the change in the house's value prior to the end of arbitration.
   c. No, because the attorney's value of the house was a reasonable estimate, not a statement of material fact.
   d. No, because the wife's lawyer agreed that the attorney's estimate of the home's value was reasonable and appropriate.

43. An attorney is in an established client-lawyer relationship with a real estate developer. The client asks the attorney for advice on how best to acquire a piece of land adjacent to their city so that the client can build two new apartment complexes on it. The land is currently zoned for agriculture but is not in use. It is adjacent to land in the city zoned for commercial use.
The attorney describes the necessary steps for purchasing the land and for appealing to the city council for a rezoning ordinance. After providing legal information, the attorney recommends against the client's plan. The attorney describes recent similar situations in which the city council has denied rezoning appeals. The client decides to purchase the land and begins appealing to the council.
Was the attorney's advice to their client appropriate?
   a. Yes, because the attorney used evidence of past cases to support their argument for what the client should do.
   b. Yes, because the attorney provided both legal information and candid advice based on their own best judgment.
   c. No, because the client chose not to follow the advice but rather to engage in a plan that may not be in their best interest.
   d. No, because the client reasonably believed that the attorney should provide only legal advice, without additional counsel.

44. A power plant's owner is called by the city council to investigate allegations that the plant is not following local and state statutes regulating air pollution. As part of this nonadjudicative proceeding, the city council asks the owner's attorney to testify. The attorney agrees and reports that the power plant is not creating illegal pollution. The attorney reasonably believes this to be true based on past conversations with their client about the business's legal requirements.

When the owner testifies, they acknowledge that the power plant is not in compliance with regulations. They state that this is due to a mechanical malfunction and that they will repair the malfunction. The city council gives them ninety days to comply with regulations.

Is the attorney subject to discipline for their testimony?
   a. Yes, because the attorney lied to the city council about a matter of substantial importance in their investigation.
   b. Yes, because the attorney was not obligated to testify during this nonadjudicative proceeding.
   c. No, because the attorney fulfilled their obligation of honest conduct in their interactions with the city council.
   d. No, because the client was not penalized by the city council for their business's pollution.

45. An attorney has been the sole legal representation for two business partners since their business's inception. One partner, Bob, is drafting his will and wants to determine the interest of his heirs in the business. The second partner, William, disagrees with Bob's proposed arrangement. Both partners agree to ask the attorney to arbitrate this dispute as a neutral third party. The attorney agrees.

After investigating the situation, the attorney meets with Bob and William and reports that they have found in Bob's favor. After the meeting, William expresses frustration with the attorney because they have a client-lawyer relationship.

Is the attorney subject to discipline?
   a. Yes, because the attorney did not inform Bob and William that they were not acting as a legal representative of either party during the arbitration.
   b. Yes, because the attorney had an obligation to William to investigate and come to an alternative solution.
   c. No, because the attorney had an obligation to honestly share their decision after investigating the conflict.
   d. No, because the attorney also had a client-lawyer relationship with Bob, which he was obliged to respect.

46. An attorney is retained as representation for a retail corporation by one of the corporation's executives. During a meeting, the executive asks the attorney for advice on designing a severance package that would most benefit the corporation during upcoming layoffs. While reviewing the proposed severance, the attorney discovers that the executive's course of action would defraud the employees of a sick time payout required by the local jurisdiction.

The attorney documents this plan to commit fraud and reports it to the board of directors. The board of directors then fires the executive for planning to commit fraud.

Is the attorney subject to discipline?
   a. Yes, because the attorney is obliged to report fraud and other illegal activities to a local authority.
   b. Yes, because the attorney did not report the fraud in the proposed severance to the executive.
   c. No, because the attorney acted in the corporation's best interest by reporting the fraud.
   d. No, because the attorney did not have a client-lawyer relationship with the executive and therefore was not obligated to act in their best interest.

103

Domain IX: Safekeeping Funds and Other Property

47. An attorney is acting as executor of their deceased client's will. The client bequeathed their house to their two heirs equally, and the heirs are in disagreement about what to do with the house. The house is being held by the attorney for safekeeping until the disagreement is resolved.

One of the heirs retains a lawyer, who contacts the attorney requesting dispersal of stocks bequeathed exclusively to that heir. The attorney declines the request because the disputed claim on the house has not yet been resolved.

Does the attorney's behavior in this matter constitute misconduct?
   a. Yes, because the attorney did not contact the heir directly after being contacted by the lawyer.
   b. Yes, because the attorney is not required to safeguard the undisputed stocks.
   c. No, because the attorney is acting according to their client's wishes to ensure both heirs are treated fairly.
   d. No, because the attorney is not taking advantage of the house in their safekeeping.

48. After forming a client-lawyer relationship with a new client, an attorney is given $10,000 by the client to hold in trust for payment of future legal fees. Over the next year, the attorney meets with the client several times to discuss the client's business interests and to provide legal advice. The attorney keeps a record of time spent with the client and time spent reviewing documentation and providing other legal services to the client. The attorney dispenses funds to their personal account based on legal services rendered.

At the end of the year, the attorney provides documentation to their client of legal fees paid from those held in trust. The client agrees that these fees are appropriate based on their agreement.

Has the attorney acted appropriately with the funds held in trust?
   a. Yes, because the attorney reasonably believed that the client's funds were intended for payment of any legal fees that accrued during the relationship.
   b. Yes, because the client confirmed that the documentation was accurate and approved dispensing the owed funds.
   c. No, because the attorney did not inform the client that they were dispensing funds from the trust account.
   d. No, because the attorney was obligated to retain the trusted funds in their personal account rather than in a second account.

49. An attorney's local jurisdiction maintains a fund for client protection. The court supports this fund by mandating an annual fee from all lawyers in the jurisdiction.

The attorney has received funds in trust from a client, and the stated purpose of those funds is to pay for the client's legal fees when working with the attorney. The attorney pays their annual fee to the court from the funds held in the trust account. When the client next requires legal services, the attorney reduces their fee by the amount previously removed from the trust account.

Is this use of the funds held in trust appropriate?
   a. Yes, because the total payment from the trust account was equal to the attorney's usual fee.
   b. Yes, because the client provided the funds for the lawyer to use as needed when paying for the client's legal fees.
   c. No, because the attorney was obligated to provide the funds to a third-party neutral to hold in trust.
   d. No, because the attorney had not provided services for which they were owed compensation at the time of the annual fee.

50. An attorney is representing the wife in a divorce case. The wife gives the attorney a box of jewelry to hold in trust during the case. The husband consents in writing to the attorney safekeeping the couple's property. The jewelry is awarded to the wife during the divorce, and the attorney dispenses the jewelry to her. The client terminates the client-lawyer relationship on good terms.

Seven years later, the ex-husband's representative contacts the attorney. The representative reports that the ex-husband is suing for a change in alimony payments. The representative requests the attorney's documentation of the value of the jewelry during the divorce. The attorney informs the representative that they shredded the documentation of the property one year ago.

Is the attorney subject to discipline?

    a. Yes, because the attorney failed to act in their client's best interest when they shredded the documentation.

    b. Yes, because the attorney has an obligation to the ex-wife, as a former client, not to provide information in the alimony case.

    c. No, because the attorney retained documentation of the jewelry for as long as was appropriate.

    d. No, because the attorney's obligation to a former client does not extend to domestic disputes.

Domain X: Communications About Legal Services

51. An attorney is beginning their independent practice and is seeking clients in order to pay their business's expenses. They visit the local court and offer their business card to any person who appears involved in legal proceedings but does not appear to currently have representation. When an individual declines, the attorney politely withdraws their solicitation.

Is the attorney subject to discipline?

    a. Yes, because the attorney is soliciting professional employment primarily with the motive of pecuniary gain.

    b. Yes, because the attorney is soliciting prospective clients who may already have representation.

    c. No, because the attorney is respecting prospective clients' wishes to not receive solicitation.

    d. No, because the attorney is soliciting at a location in which they reasonably believe most individuals may need legal services.

52. An attorney contacts a social club in their city, offering a reduced rate to members of the club who are interested in retaining legal services. The social club's officer informs the attorney that their offer may interest the membership. The officer emails the attorney's information to members of the club.

As a result of this solicitation, the attorney is contacted by five prospective clients. Of those, two individuals opt to form a client-lawyer relationship with the attorney.

Was this attorney's solicitation appropriate?

    a. No, because the attorney solicited an individual who they did not reasonably believe was in need of legal services.

    b. No, because the attorney engaged in an inappropriate person-to-person solicitation with a prospective client.

    c. Yes, because the attorney formed a client-lawyer relationship with the social club prior to soliciting its membership.

    d. Yes, because soliciting an organization in this way constitutes advertising rather than person-to-person contact.

105

53. A law firm that specializes in personal injury law produces a television commercial advertising its services. The commercial encourages anyone who has been in a car accident to contact the firm to discuss their insurance claim for medical bills or property damage. The commercial advertises the law firm's consistent past track record of successful litigation for personal injuries.
Does this commercial follow the requirements for professional conduct in advertising legal services?
   a. Yes, because the commercial's argument relies upon the material fact of the law firm's past successes.
   b. Yes, because the commercial is directed at a general audience and thus is not soliciting a specific person.
   c. No, because the law firm uses misleading claims when encouraging prospective clients to call.
   d. No, because the law firm specializes in personal injury law, not in litigating medical insurance claims.

54. An attorney who specializes in domestic disputes and divorce cases frequently suggests the use of an escrow agent to their clients. When asked by a client, the attorney consistently recommends the same escrow agent. The attorney reasonably believes that escrow agent is the best in their city. The escrow agent, in turn, recommends the attorney's legal services when they are appropriate and reasonable for a prospective client's needs. Neither professional has made a formal agreement regarding this referral practice.
Is the attorney subject to discipline for referring clients to the escrow agent?
   a. Yes, because neither professional has sought an exclusive referral arrangement.
   b. Yes, because the attorney has not sought an exclusive referral arrangement.
   c. No, because the attorney reasonably believes the escrow agent provides the best local escrow service.
   d. No, because neither professional has sought an exclusive referral arrangement.

55. An attorney takes out an advertisement in a local newspaper. The advertisement emphasizes the attorney's services pertaining to representing the defendant in criminal cases. The advertisement also claims that the attorney is a specialist in labor and employment law. The attorney is certified by an accredited agency with authority to certify lawyers in their state. The advertisement includes the certifying agency's name at the bottom of the listing.
Does this advertisement violate professional standards?
   a. Yes, because the attorney's certification misleads the reader about their expertise.
   b. Yes, because the advertisement does not indicate whether or not the attorney is a member of a law firm.
   c. No, because the attorney has provided all requisite information about their specialist certification.
   d. No, because the advertisement primarily advertises legal services for criminal law, not civil law.

Domain XI: Lawyers' Duties to the Public and the Legal System

56. An attorney serves on a local committee that provides grants to low-income individuals to help them pay for legal services. The attorney is part of the decision-making process. He is neither the organization's representative nor in a client-lawyer relationship with any member of the organization. The committee receives a grant request from the defendant in a criminal case alleging theft from the defendant's employer. The attorney represents the defendant's spouse in matters related to the couple's side business operating a family farm. When the grant request is brought before the committee, the attorney recuses themselves from the decision.

Was the attorney's decision appropriate?

    a. Yes, because the attorney is obliged not to participate in a decision that may be materially adverse to their client's best interests.

    b. Yes, because the attorney reasonably believes they are biased toward denying the defendant's request for a grant.

    c. No, because the attorney is obliged to advocate for the defendant as the defendant's representation through the relationship with their spouse.

    d. No, because as a member of the committee, the attorney is obliged to participate in all grant-distribution decisions.

57. An attorney financially contributes to the election campaign of their state's incumbent governor, and the governor wins. Two years into the governor's new term, the state's prior attorney general retires. The governor nominates the attorney as the new attorney general. Multiple lawyers without political affiliation vouch for the attorney's competence and professional conduct. The attorney's nomination is approved by the state legislature, and the attorney accepts the position.

Is the attorney subject to discipline?

    a. Yes, because it's reasonable to believe that the attorney made their campaign contribution in exchange for a nomination.

    b. Yes, because the attorney is obligated to decline the position.

    c. No, because the attorney did not contribute to the campaign for the purpose of obtaining the position of attorney general.

    d. No, because the attorney's professional conduct was attested to by politically neutral lawyers.

Domain XII: Judicial Conduct

58. An attorney receives a request from the attorney general's office to anonymously evaluate a judge in their district. The attorney is a prosecutor and works with the judge frequently. The attorney considers the judge a personal friend, and they spend time together during public and private events. Privately, however, the attorney does not believe that the judge is competent to preside over trials concerning recent legislation about digital crimes.

During the evaluation, the attorney gives an honest account of the judge's professional strengths. They also describe their concerns about the judge's familiarity with modern technology.

Was the attorney's evaluation of the judge appropriate?

    a. Yes, because it's reasonable that the attorney general's office knew that the attorney is a prosecutor and likely has a close relationship with the judge.

    b. Yes, because the attorney disclosed their private concerns about the judge during the evaluation.

    c. No, because the attorney did not disclose their personal relationship with the judge during the evaluation.

    d. No, because it's reasonable to believe the attorney's account of the judge's strengths was purposed to retain a judge who is not professionally impartial.

59. A judge receives a request for an *ex parte* hearing by a tenant to deny the owner's sale of the house. The tenant is in an ongoing eviction case with the property owner. The jurisdiction requires that notice of the *ex parte* hearing be given to the other party one day before it is submitted. The tenant has completed this requirement, and the property owner has not appeared for the hearing.

During the hearing, the judge listens to the argument made by the tenant's lawyer, reviews the tenant's documentation, and concludes that the motion to deny the sale of the house until the eviction case is resolved is just. The judge orders that the owner may not sell the property until the eviction case is resolved.

Was the judge's treatment of the tenant and the property owner professionally appropriate?

    a. Yes, because the tenant provided the required notification to the property owner prior to the hearing.

    b. Yes, because the judge reviewed all materials that were provided at the *ex parte* hearing and made a decision based on those materials.

    c. No, because the judge did not step in and advocate for the property owner in the place of their own representation.

    d. No, because the judge did not ask the tenant's lawyer to provide all relevant material facts regardless of whether they were adverse to the tenant.

60. A judge is invited to join a new organization in their community that aims to improve educational outcomes in the area and provide greater access to lifelong learning. The organization asks the judge to review the drafted bylaws of the organization and provide legal guidance on a volunteer basis. The judge agrees.

The next year, a person who was the defendant in a civil court case that the judge presided over is elected to the organization's board of directors. The judge is also elected to the board of directors. The judge does not have a client-lawyer relationship with the individual, and the civil court case was resolved three years ago.

Is it appropriate for the judge to continue volunteering their legal services to this organization?

    a. Yes, because the past court case does not hinder the judge's impartiality in their current obligations.

    b. Yes, because the judge has agreed to provide a substantial service to their community, thereby bolstering the prestige of the legal profession.

    c. No, because the judge should avoid all professional and private intercourse with persons involved in court cases over which they have presided.

    d. No, because the judge may not provide volunteer legal advice to a person previously involved in a court case over which they presided.

Answer Explanations #2

Domain I: Regulation of the Legal Profession

1. C: Choice *C* is correct because any person who is neither part of the applicant's household nor a fellow student can provide an affidavit of good character (such as a minister or a professor) so long as they are familiar with the applicant. Choices *A* and *D* are incorrect because the applicant's relationship with the attorney's partner does not impact whether or not the attorney can provide her with an affidavit. Choice *B* is incorrect because familiarity with the applicant in a legal context is not required.

2. B: Choice *B* is correct because the absence of the defendant's signature on the settlement offer in combination with the lawyer's explanation provides the attorney with reason to believe the defendant's lawyer is not authorized to make this offer. This constitutes misconduct, which ought to be reported to a professional authority. Choice *A* is incorrect because it is plausible that the lawyer truly believed they were acting in their client's best interest. Choice *C* is incorrect because the rules for misconduct are the same in both civil and criminal trials. Choice *D* is incorrect because a lawyer's sincere belief that an action is in the client's best interest does not excuse misconduct.

3. D: Choice *D* is correct because Rule 5.5 of the ABA's *Model Rules of Professional Conduct* permits working outside the attorney's jurisdiction so long as they do so in association with a lawyer licensed to practice in that jurisdiction. By working with the Georgian lawyer, the attorney is complying with professional standards. Choice *A* is incorrect because Rule 5.5 lists this situation as a circumstance in which the attorney may practice law outside Florida. Choice *B* is incorrect because the client's wish to maintain an existing relationship does not allow the attorney to ignore legal or professional requirements related to the practice of law. Choice *C* is incorrect because the *lack* of county-level restrictions does not logically override the general restriction that the attorney may only practice law where they are licensed to do so.

4. D: While a lawyer may accept fees that are contingent on the outcome of a case (such as successfully winning an insurance claim), they may not do so in domestic proceedings if the fee is contingent on the amount of alimony awarded. Thus, Choice *D* is correct. Choice *A* is incorrect because the attorney engaged in misconduct by agreeing to the contingent bonus fee. Choice *B* is incorrect because the attorney's investigation has no bearing on whether or not accepting this fee was misconduct. Choice *C* is incorrect because the question provides no reasonable indication that the attorney was in a client-lawyer relationship with the ex-husband.

5. C: Restrictions on the right for a lawyer to practice law is forbidden in all settlements; therefore, the lawyer should decline the offer. Even though accepting the terms of the offer, as in Choices *A* and *B*, may have achieved their client's objectives, doing so would constitute malpractice since the offer would restrict the attorney from practicing law. While the terms of this offer cannot be accepted, this situation does not warrant a complete withdrawal from the case, as in Choice *D*.

Domain II: The Client-Lawyer Relationship

6. A: Choice *A* is correct because it's considered unprofessional to charge more than other attorneys in the same locality for services that are of a similar complexity and require a similar level of expertise. Choice *B* is incorrect because a formal consult is not required when setting one's fee, only that the fee is reasonable for the locality. Choice *C* is incorrect because the nearby city is far enough away and the difference in fee is large enough that it can't reasonably be considered part of the attorney's locality.

110

Choice D is incorrect because a fee of $400 per hour is about double the current average of the city's representative fees listed in the question (about $200 per hour). This new fee is not considered reasonable.

7. B: Choice B is correct because the objectives of a client-lawyer relationship are defined by the client, and in rejecting the offer immediately, the attorney did not abide by their client's wishes. The attorney should have communicated with the client to confirm whether they were willing to compromise on their monetary goal in exchange for a quick resolution to the case. Choice A is incorrect because since the settlement offer was lower than the client's goal, the attorney did not have implicit authority to accept the offer. Choice C is incorrect because acting in a client's best interest does not justify an attorney acting against their client's objectives in a case. Choice D is incorrect because rejecting the offer was not within the scope of the attorney's authority.

8. C: Choice C is correct because an attorney is obligated to terminate their relationship with a client if that client seeks to use the attorney's services to commit fraud, break the law, or commit another illegal or immoral act. Choice A is incorrect because in this situation, the attorney is not obligated to act in the client's best interest. Choice B is incorrect because the attorney was not obliged to inform an authority prior to informing the factory; however, she does *now* have an obligation to do so since the violations have continued after she informed the factory. Choice D is incorrect because the situation does not state that the client-lawyer relationship was terminated by the client, it was terminated by the attorney.

9. C: Choice C is correct because with an established client, it is reasonable for the attorney to believe that they know when the client is joking and when they are serious. The attorney has no substantial reason to believe that the client will burn down the building to commit insurance fraud. Thus, Choice A is incorrect. Choice B is also incorrect because discussing hypothetical situations is an important aspect of *avoiding* fraud when counseling a client. Choice D is incorrect because an attorney is indeed obligated to avoid indirect requests to commit fraud. In this case, however, the attorney reasonably believes that the client is not making an inappropriate indirect request.

10. B: The attorney acted within his apparent authority as the will's executor by determining details left unspecified in the document (such as the time and place in which it would be read). Thus, Choice B is correct. Choice A is incorrect because this answer does not describe why the attorney had the authority to make this decision. Choice C is incorrect because the attorney had apparent authority due to being the executor. Choice D is incorrect because the situation does not provide reason to believe the child had actual authority, in particular because they were not a beneficiary of the will.

11. A: An attorney may not solicit a person if that person has already expressed that they do not want to form a client-lawyer relationship. Thus, Choice A is correct. Choice B is incorrect because offering to do *pro bono* work is not considered unprofessional. Choice C is incorrect because while solicitation is permissible in some circumstances if a lawyer is not seeking pecuniary gain, this does not make repeated solicitation permissible. Choice D is incorrect because repeated solicitations still constitute misconduct regardless of whether the attorney reasonably believes this.

12. B: Choice B is correct because this answer accurately describes the attorney's duty to the employee as one of their former clients in a case against this factory. Choice A is incorrect because the attorney is permitted to represent the factory in circumstances outside of labor relations (for example, a claim against the factory's insurance provider). Choice C is incorrect because the members of a class action lawsuit are each considered former clients of the attorney. Choice D is incorrect because while the

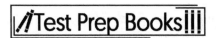

manager is the one contacting the attorney, the prospective client is the factory as a legal entity (or the factory's owner, its corporation, etc.).

13. D: Choice *D* is correct because in this situation, the attorney reasonably believes that they do not have the information desired by the client. Their brief response and offer to discuss further is appropriate. Choice *A* is incorrect because the attorney has not failed in this obligation. Choice *B* is incorrect because the attorney does not reasonably have a complete answer to provide. Choice *C* is incorrect because answering a client's question at the start of the case doesn't logically preclude the same question from being relevant later in the case (although in this case, the question is not substantially important).

Domain III: Client Confidentiality

14. A: Information protected by attorney-client privilege remains privileged unless it is released by the client or with their informed consent in writing. Since the corporation has not approved releasing this draft offer, the attorney must abide by attorney-client privilege concerning it. Thus, Choice *A* is correct, and Choices *C* and *D* are incorrect. Choice *B* is incorrect because some aspects of this case are not protected by attorney-client privilege (for example, the names of plaintiffs identified in the case).

15. C: Choice *C* is correct because one of the circumstances in which an attorney must breach attorney-client privilege and report confidential information is when the attorney reasonably believes there is a risk of bodily harm. The client's confession and expressed desire provide sufficient reason to believe she may attempt to harm her ex-boyfriend in the future. Choice *A* is incorrect because the protection against double jeopardy does not restrict the attorney's actions as a private citizen. Choice *B* is incorrect because knowing the planned method is not necessary for the attorney to reasonably believe, based on the evidence of past actions, that their client would make another attempt. Choice *D* is incorrect because former clients are still protected by confidentiality.

16. D: The client consented to the release of confidential information to their religious authority. The attorney followed the client's directions and is not reasonably responsible for the religious authority's actions. Thus, Choice *D* is correct. Choice *A* is incorrect because a lawyer's confidentiality requirements do not take into account another person's profession. Choice *B* is incorrect because the attorney is not responsible for emotional harm done by a person to whom the client consented to release confidential information. Choice *C* is incorrect because a religious authority's confidentiality requirements are not logically relevant to whether or not a lawyer may share a client's confidential information.

17. B: Choice *B* is correct because the work-product doctrine places the burden of proof on the prosecution in this case. The prosecution is required to prove that the requested documentation is necessary for their case before the attorney is mandated to provide the affidavits. Choice *A* is incorrect because the prosecution is requesting documentation, not a deposition regarding conversations between the attorney and the client. Choice *C* is incorrect because the attorney is obligated to challenge the request in order to act in the client's best interests. Choice *D* is incorrect because the notarization of a document does not preclude that document from being considered confidential.

18. B: Choice *B* is correct because scheduling this meeting is a situation in which the attorney can reasonably infer their client's consent to the disclosure since doing so does not reasonably create a risk of bodily harm and furthers the client's best interests by getting the meeting scheduled. Since implicit consent is permissible when disclosing a client's location, Choice *A* is incorrect. Choices *C* and *D* are

112

incorrect because a client's location is always considered confidential, even if it's less important than most confidential client information.

Domain IV: Conflicts of Interest

19. A: Choice *A* is correct because the attorney has equal obligations of loyalty and confidentiality to each client when jointly representing multiple clients in the same case. The attorney is obligated to disclose all information that is pertinent to the case to the other clients. Choice *B* is incorrect because the attorney is not obligated to share confidential, non-pertinent information (for example, advice given to one of the clients concerning firing an employee for a reason unrelated to this regulatory case). Choice *C* is incorrect because in joint representation, the disclosed information must be disclosed to the other clients. Choice *D* is incorrect because the shared information *is* pertinent to the other clients' involvement in this case.

20. D: Choice *D* is correct because the house was sold at a fair market rate, and thus the attorney was only obliged to seek the client's informed consent about the transaction in writing. Choice *A* is incorrect because this situation describes circumstances in which a lawyer is permitted to engage in a business transaction with a client. Choice *B* is incorrect because the attorney was not required to *force* the client to seek other representation so long as the client acknowledged their right to do so and consented to the attorney's continued representation. Choice *C* is incorrect because accepting a business transaction that benefits the attorney does not constitute acting in the client's best interest, even if the client made the offer.

21. C: An attorney may not take a client whose interests are opposed to a former client in regard to the same matter in which the attorney represented the former client. While the spouse's interests are opposed to the former client's interests, the divorce case is not substantially similar to the lawsuit for unpaid PTO. Thus, Choice *C* is correct, and Choice *B* is incorrect. Choice *A* is incorrect because the attorney had a duty to not use information learned while representing the former client against him in this case. Choice *D* is incorrect because a successful case does not excuse potential misconduct.

22. A: Choice *A* is correct because as a member of the firm, the attorney is not permitted to form a client-lawyer relationship with anyone whose interests are opposed to the plaintiff represented by the firm. Thus, Choice *C* is incorrect. Choice *B* is incorrect because it is reasonable to believe that the attorney is indeed an expert in personal injury law. Choice *D* is incorrect because providing testimony in exchange for a fee does adversely affect the firm's client even if the attorney does not actually join the defendant's legal team.

23. D: Choice *D* is correct because the attorney had a pecuniary interest in the outcome of the case. Although the attorney reasonably acted in their client's best interests rather than in the attorney's interest as a stockholder, the attorney still engaged in misconduct by not disclosing their interest to the employee. Thus, Choices *A* and *B* are incorrect. Choice *C* is incorrect because the attorney did not have the stated obligation.

24. A: Choice *A* is correct because the attorney used confidential information they received during the case to make a purchase that would provide them with financial benefit. This constitutes acquiring an inappropriate interest in the litigation. Choice *B* is incorrect because the CEO's plans for growth do not reasonably constitute a plan to establish an illegal monopoly. Choice *C* is incorrect because the attorney sold the land to the construction company for their own benefit. Choice *D* is incorrect because the

113

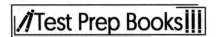
attorney made the decision based on information disclosed to them as part of their client-lawyer relationship.

25. C: Choice *C* is correct because the judge acted as a mediator and thus can't represent either man in the divorce proceeding. Thus, Choices *A* and *D* are incorrect. The judge did have a right to receive compensation for mediation even though it was unsuccessful. Thus, Choice *B* is incorrect.

26. D: The law clerk, like the judge, is considered a third-party neutral for this case. They were obligated to inform the judge that they were seeking employment, and according to Rule 1.12b of the *Model Rules of Professional Conduct,* the law clerk is permitted to seek or accept employment at the defendant's firm. This is permissible because the law clerk does not have a client-lawyer relationship with either party in the case. Thus, Choices *A* and *B* are incorrect. Choice *C* is incorrect because neither the lawyer nor the law clerk is subject to discipline. Furthermore, if the lawyer had engaged in misconduct, that would not logically preclude the possibility that the law clerk may have engaged in misconduct and been subject to discipline.

27. D: If all parties agree and sign a formal agreement, the attorney can still represent the client. In this situation, all parties may have verbally agreed to the proposed representation, as described in Choice *A,* but because there may be confidential information that could be used in the case, they need to write and sign the agreement before representation can take place. Choice *B* is incorrect because it's missing the necessary formal, written agreement. Choice *C* is incorrect because there are exceptions.

Domain V: Competence, Legal Malpractice, and Other Civil Liability

28. C: Despite having written documentation that the client does not intend to sue, the attorney was still obligated to report the potential malpractice claim to their insurance provider. Thus, Choice *C* is correct. Choice *A* is incorrect because they did not report the liability. Choice *B* is incorrect because the client's statement does not constitute waiving their right to sue. Choice *D* is incorrect because if the attorney had been appropriately diligent, their client's case would not have passed the statute of limitations.

29. B: Choice *B* is correct because the attorney was "exploring" the use of an AI program. This reasonably indicates that the attorney is not competent with the technology; therefore, using the program constitutes a lack of due diligence on the part of the attorney. Choice *A* is incorrect because an attorney is not required to devise a closing argument wholly on their own (for example, other members of the legal team may assist). Choice *C* is incorrect because an actual case is not an appropriate environment in which to practice using a new technology. Choice *D* is incorrect because the program's relevance does not logically imply that the attorney is competent to use the new technology in a courtroom.

30. A: Choice *A* is correct because the attorney showed due diligence by preparing for a reasonably possible emergency in creating this plan. Choice *B* is incorrect because the attorney was not obliged to maintain the client-lawyer relationship after retirement. Choice *C* is incorrect because the attorney is only obligated to be prepared for a crisis. They are not required to terminate the client-lawyer relationship. Choice *D* is incorrect because reaching out to established contacts is a reasonable course of action when formulating this type of plan.

31. C: Choice *C* is correct because the attorney's familial relationships provide reasonable grounds for the attorney to recognize personal bias if they were to attempt to represent the defendant. Choice *A* is

114

incorrect because a lawyer is not obliged to represent causes they find repugnant, especially if their personal beliefs are likely to hinder the client-lawyer relationship. Thus, Choice *B* is also incorrect. Choice *D* is incorrect because competence is indeed logically associated with the ability to represent a client—the attorney declined, not because of incompetence, but because they would be unable to use their competence with due diligence.

32. D: Choice *D* is correct because no agreement should limit a lawyer's liability for having breached the *Model Rules of Professional Conduct.* Overlooking relevant information constitutes malpractice due to incompetence, for which a lawyer shall not make an agreement to prospectively limit their liability. Regardless of whether malpractice occurred during this trial, this liability section was still inappropriate. Choice *A* is incorrect because while the statement is accurate, it does not pertinently address the stipulations in the liability section. Choice *B* is incorrect because the client's consent does not allow the attorney to behave unprofessionally. Choice *C* is incorrect because regardless of the suit, including a liability section that allows for gross negligence from the lawyer is unacceptable.

33. C: Choice *C* is correct because it is reasonable to infer from the description of their activities that the attorney has not renewed their license. In most states, a lawyer must renew their license annually or biannually. Thus, even though Minnesota's renewal period is not stated, it is reasonable to infer from the three-year requirement for continuing education that the attorney is overdue for renewing their license. Thus, Choice *A* is also incorrect. Choice *B* is incorrect because a lawyer does not need to have engaged in malpractice to be found incompetent. Choice *D* is incorrect because the attorney has completed the requisite hours of ethics education; they have *not* completed the requisite hours of elimination of bias education.

Domain VI: Litigation and Other Forms of Advocacy

34. A: Choice *A* is correct because all legal professionals have an obligation to expedite litigation in good faith. The child's birthday was not a reasonable cause for delaying the trial. Thus, Choice *C* is also incorrect. Choice *B* is incorrect because the attorney did not seek to impact the trial's outcome by the delay. Choice *D* is incorrect because a lawyer may not breach the *Model Rules of Professional Conduct* nor advocate for a client's interests in a dishonest way.

35. C: Choice *C* is correct because the camera's placement across the street implies that the defendant's claim that they did not consent to surveillance is frivolous as the employer did not own the camera and the camera was surveilling a public space. Choice *A* is incorrect because an attorney is not obligated to make frivolous claims. Choice *B* is incorrect because the described security camera does not reasonably constitute workplace surveillance. Choice *D* is incorrect because the attorney is obligated to contest evidence, but only if doing so is not frivolous.

36. B: Choice *B* is correct because the lost property's minimal value is a plausible objection to the relevance of the testimony to the witness's character. Choice *A* is incorrect because the described situation does not logically lead one to conclude that the attorney is attempting to intentionally frustrate the defense. Thus, Choice *D* is also incorrect. The judge's denial of the objection does not necessarily indicate that the attorney didn't make the objection in good faith. Thus, Choice *C* is incorrect because the testimony's relevance doesn't imply the objection was frivolous.

37. C: During an *ex parte* proceeding, if representatives from both sides of a case are not present, it is the responsibility of those present to provide the judge or tribunal with all pertinent information so that they can make an informed decision as quickly as possible. The attorney acted in good faith in providing

the judge with pertinent information. Thus, Choice *C* is correct. Choice *A* is incorrect because the attorney did act in their client's best interest by advocating for their goals professionally. Choice *B* is incorrect because the attorney was not obligated to insist that the wife's representation be present. Choice *D* is incorrect because the husband's request for a temporary restraining order was not successful.

38. A: Choice *A* is correct because the attorney has stated a matter of public record and has not disclosed confidential information to the reporter. Choice *B* is incorrect because an attorney is obliged to conceal confidential information (such as evidence that may be used in the trial). Choice *C* is incorrect because there is no obligation to speak only during an official conference. Choice *D* is incorrect because while the attorney did confirm the accusation, this did not warrant discipline since the accusation is a matter of public record.

39. B: According to Rule 3.7 of the *Model Rules of Professional Conduct*, if a lawyer reasonably believes that they will be called as a witness to testify about substantial matters in a case, that lawyer should not act as the client's advocate during the trial. Thus, Choice *B* is correct. Choice *A* is incorrect because the attorney has an obligation to testify if called although they are not obligated to divulge confidential information pertinent to the case. Choices *C* and *D* are incorrect because the attorney's truthfulness is not pertinent to their misconduct in this situation.

Domain VII: Transactions and Communications with Persons Other Than Clients

40. D: The attorney may not communicate with Harry about the civil case against the retail store without the consent of Harry's lawyer. Choice *D* is correct because Harry's question about the personal injury case is not a subject for which Harry is already receiving representation. Choice *A* is incorrect because the attorney is only obliged not to communicate with Harry directly about the case in which Harry is already represented. Choice *B* is incorrect because giving Harry this recommendation does not infringe on the client-lawyer relationship the attorney has with Jen. Choice *C* is incorrect because the lawyer is *not* permitted to advise both plaintiffs without the consent of Harry's representation.

41. B: Choice *B* is correct because the attorney was obliged to notify their client immediately about the business partner's documents on the drive. Informing the client two weeks later constitutes misconduct. Thus, Choice *C* is also incorrect. Choice *A* is incorrect because the attorney's obligation in this case is to notify the *sender*, not the business partner, per Rule 4.4(b) of the *Model Rules of Professional Conduct*. Choice *D* is incorrect because the attorney had no reason to assume the business partner had consented to the sharing of their financial documents with the attorney.

Domain VIII: Different Roles of the Lawyer

42. C: Choice *C* is correct because a lawyer's obligation to honest statements in negotiation extends primarily to statements of material fact. Because the attorney both estimated the house's value and *stated* that it was an estimate, they were acting in good faith. Choice *A* is incorrect because making an erroneous estimate does not constitute dishonesty. Choice *B* is incorrect because there is no reason to believe that the attorney knew the house's value would increase. Choice *D* is incorrect because the attorney's honesty is not contingent on another lawyer's agreement with their statements (for example, one lawyer colluding with another lawyer's false statement by asserting that it was accurate would constitute dishonesty).

43. B: Choice *B* is correct because a lawyer is obligated to make both their legal expertise and their honest judgment of other factors available to their client when acting as an advisor. Choice *A* is incorrect

116

because the attorney was providing advice, not structuring an argument—a lawyer's objective is not to persuade a client to act a certain way. Rather, their duty is to provide all of the information necessary for the client to make an informed decision. Thus, Choice *C* is also incorrect since the client is free to make their own choices regardless of their best interest. Choice *D* is incorrect because it is not reasonable to infer from the situation that the client wanted strictly legal information devoid of the attorney's reasoned opinion.

44. C: The attorney had a professional obligation to provide honest testimony to the tribunal and did so to the best of their ability. Choice *C* is correct. Choice *A* is incorrect because although the attorney was incorrect, they reasonably believed their statement to be true. Choice *B* is incorrect because the attorney was obligated to assist the tribunal's investigation. Choice *D* is incorrect because whether or not the attorney's statement harmed the client's interests is not relevant to the evaluation of their conduct when assisting a valid legal authority.

45. A: Choice *A* is correct because a lawyer, when acting as a neutral third party, must always inform all parties that they are not representing anyone. Choice *B* is incorrect because if the attorney reasonably believed Bob's proposed arrangement was best, they had an obligation to support that arrangement. Choice *C* is incorrect because the attorney is subject to discipline for the reason presented above regardless of the fact that they fulfilled their obligation to investigate the conflict and honestly share their decision. Choice *D* is incorrect because the attorney was obligated, in acting as a third-party neutral, to act without regard to *either* client-lawyer relationship.

46. B: Choice *B* is correct because while the attorney is obligated to report illegal activity to a higher authority in the corporation, the executive has not yet committed fraud. It is plausible that the executive did not know the proposed severance constituted fraud. Thus, the attorney was obligated to report the fraud first to the executive before seeking a higher corporate or legal authority. Thus, Choices *A* and *D* are also incorrect. Choice *C* is incorrect because addressing the fraud with the executive first would have been in the corporation's best interest.

Domain IX: Safekeeping Funds and Other Property
47. B: Choice *B* is correct because the attorney, when safekeeping property in this situation, is only obligated to handle property that is disputed by the two heirs. Choice *A* is incorrect because communicating with a person's legal representative is appropriate. Choice *C* is incorrect because it is not reasonable to believe that the deceased client wanted the attorney to safeguard *all* property until any disputes were resolved. Choice *D* is incorrect because, while the attorney's handling of the house is appropriate, their handling of the stocks is inappropriate.

48. A: Choice *A* is correct because the attorney utilized the funds for their intended purpose and later provided all relevant information pertaining to the use of the funds to the client. Choice *B* is incorrect because the client was provided documentation of *past* dispensation, not asked to approve a *future* dispensation. Choice *C* is incorrect because the attorney reasonably believed they were not obligated to inform the client of dispensation due to the ongoing relationship. Choice *D* is incorrect because a lawyer should avoid combining personal property with property held in safekeeping, including funds provided for the payment of future legal fees.

49. D: Choice *D* is correct because the attorney used the trust account to pay a fee against their future compensation. This is inappropriate because the client's funds were not given for use in that circumstance. Choice *A* is incorrect because the use of the funds still constitutes misconduct even if the

117

client's expenditure remained the same. Choice *B* is incorrect because the court's annual fee does not constitute the client's legal fees. Choice *C* is incorrect because a lawyer may hold their client's funds in trust—they are not obligated to give them to an escrow agent or another third-party neutral.

50. C: Choice *C* is correct because an attorney is required to maintain records of property held in safekeeping for at least five years after the end of the client-lawyer relationship. Since the attorney shredded the documentation six years after the end of the relationship, they have met their professional obligation. Choice *A* is incorrect because the attorney was not obligated to retain the documentation beyond five years. Choice *B* is incorrect because complying with a reasonable request for information does not constitute adverse harm to a former client's interests. Choice *D* is incorrect because the attorney does have an obligation to provide documentation to a former client in any case, including domestic disputes.

Domain X: Communications About Legal Services

51. A: Choice *A* is correct because per Rule 7.3(b) of the *Model Rules of Professional Conduct,* a lawyer may not solicit professional employment live person-to-person when financial gain is the major motive for that lawyer. Choice *B* is incorrect because the attorney is only soliciting persons they reasonably believe are not currently represented. Choices *C* and *D* are incorrect because these reasons do not justify the attorney soliciting for the sake of financially supporting their new business.

52. D: Choice *D* is correct because a lawyer may contact a group to offer it a special deal, discount, etc. for legal services. This is considered advertising (like paying for a billboard advertisement), not direct, person-to-person solicitation. Thus, Choice *A* is incorrect. Choice *B* is incorrect because the attorney contacted the officer as a representative of the organization, not as an individual being solicited as a prospective client. Choice *C* is incorrect because the attorney did not take the club, as an organization, as a client.

53. C: Choice *C* is correct because the law firm's claim to litigate both *medical bills* and *property damage* is misleading since the firm uses its past record of the former as a key advertising point. Thus, Choices *A* and *B* are also incorrect because these accurate statements do not justify the misleading claim. Choice *D* is incorrect because personal injury law does overlap with litigating medical insurance claims.

54. D: A lawyer may mutually refer prospective clients to another legal or non-legal professional when a reasonable person would believe retaining that professional's services is truly in the client's best interest. However, a lawyer may *not* enter into an agreement to refer clients exclusively to a specific professional who provides said service. Thus, Choice *D* is correct, and Choices *A* and *B* are incorrect. Choice *C* is incorrect because the quality of the escrow agent does not explain why the consistent pattern of referrals is appropriate.

55. C: Choice *C* is correct because while the attorney's certified specialty in labor and employment law is not relevant for an advertisement about criminal defense law, publishing an ineffective advertisement does not violate the *Model Rules of Professional Conduct.* Thus, Choice *D* is also incorrect. Choice *A* is incorrect because a reasonable person would not be misled about the attorney since the certifying agency is listed, and a reasonable person would not equate criminal defense law with labor and employment law. Choice *B* is incorrect because an independent attorney isn't required to say they're *not* a member in a law firm.

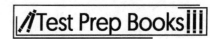

Domain XI: Lawyers' Duties to the Public and the Legal System

56. A: Choice *A* is correct because a lawyer participating in a legal organization may not partake in any decisions of that organization that could be adverse to a client's interests. Choice *B* is incorrect because the attorney is likely biased toward *accepting* the defendant's request, not denying it. Choice *C* is incorrect because the attorney is not obliged to advocate for the defendant as a member of the committee. Choice *D* is incorrect because the attorney has an obligation to recuse themselves from this decision.

57. C: A reasonable person can infer from this situation that the attorney's campaign contribution was not personally motivated since the prior attorney general remained in their position for another two years following the contribution. Participating in political activities—including financial contributions—is a protected activity that a lawyer may engage in. Thus, Choice *C* is correct, and Choice *A* is incorrect. Choice *B* is incorrect because the attorney is only required to decline the position if obtaining the position was a substantial motive in making the contribution. Choice *D* is incorrect because while the attestations to the attorney's character do help validate that the attorney's contribution was not made to obtain the position, such testimony does not necessarily indicate that the attorney acted professionally in this case.

Domain XII: Judicial Conduct

58. B: Choice *B* is correct because the attorney did not allow any personal biases to interfere with their professional opinion. This is an important element in continuing to ensure the impartiality, competence, and diligence of judges in the judicial system despite the close relationships that may occur during legal work. Choice *A* is incorrect because the attorney general's knowledge does not therefore indicate that *any* testimony the attorney gave would be appropriate. Choice *C* is incorrect because it is reasonable to believe that the attorney general's office knew of the professional and working relationship between the attorney and the judge. Choice *D* is incorrect because the situation described gives no plausible reason to believe that the judge's incompetence concerning digital legislation is due to partiality or bias.

59. D: Choice *D* is correct because in an *ex parte* hearing, the judge and the lawyer have a professional obligation to ensure that the result of the hearing is both substantive and just. A lawyer may be required to provide information or documentation that is adverse to the interests of their client in the greater interest of ensuring justice is performed. In turn, the judge had an obligation to ensure the property owner's position was considered during the hearing even if their representative was not present. Choice *A* is incorrect because the tenant's correct behavior does not free the judge of their obligation. Choice *B* is incorrect because no mention is made of arguments or documentation made in the opposing party's favor. Choice *C* is incorrect because a judge may not act as an advocate for a single side of a case even if they lack representation. The judge was obliged to remain neutral.

60. A: Choice *A* is correct because the judge does not currently have a professional relationship with the former defendant. It is appropriate for them to interact with this individual in a community setting. Choice *B* is incorrect because while bolstering the legal profession's prestige in the community is a good objective, seeking or attaining that objective would not justify improper behavior. Choice *C* is incorrect because a judge does not have to avoid all contact with persons involved in court cases over which they've presided. Choice *D* is incorrect because providing the organization with legal guidance does not constitute forming a client-lawyer relationship with this individual.

Dear MPRE Test Taker,

Thank you for purchasing this study guide for your MPRE exam. We hope that we exceeded your expectations.

Our goal in creating this study guide was to cover all of the topics that you will see on the test. We also strove to make our practice questions as similar as possible to what you will encounter on test day. With that being said, if you found something that you feel was not up to your standards, please send us an email and let us know.

We have study guides in a wide variety of fields. If the one you are looking for isn't listed above, then try searching for it on Amazon or send us an email.

Thanks Again and Happy Testing!
Product Development Team
info@studyguideteam.com

FREE Test Taking Tips Video/DVD Offer

To better serve you, we created videos covering test taking tips that we want to give you for FREE. **These videos cover world-class tips that will help you succeed on your test.**

We just ask that you send us feedback about this product. Please let us know what you thought about it—whether good, bad, or indifferent.

To get your **FREE videos**, you can use the QR code below or email freevideos@studyguideteam.com with "Free Videos" in the subject line and the following information in the body of the email:

a. The title of your product

b. Your product rating on a scale of 1-5, with 5 being the highest

c. Your feedback about the product

If you have any questions or concerns, please don't hesitate to contact us at info@studyguideteam.com.

Thank you!